W9-CCN-450
GOYA
Chick Peas
Garbanzos
GULDEN'S
CHARMS
Fluffy Stuff
Cotton Candy
Betty Crocker
Rich & Creamy
PURE SESAME OIL
PRODUCT OF JAPAN
56 FL.OZ.(1656ml)
KADOYA SESAME MILLS INC.
CENTO
TOMATO PASTE
Classic
Reese's
PEANUT BUTTER CUPS
Miniatures
Jif
Honey Maid
8g of whole grain
Honey
Wondra
QUICK-MIXING FLOUR
ALL-PURPOSE
TOLL HOUSE
Nestle
SEMI-SWEET MORSELS
Valentina
MAILLE
Dijon Originale
SCLAFANI
CRUSHED TOMATOES
BA-TAMPTE
KEEP REFRIGERATED
Half Sour
Pickles
32 FL. OZ. (1 QT.) 946 L
SESAME SEED
SHAVED TRUFFLES
BLACK TRUFFLE OLIVE OIL
SWEET BABY RAY'S
The Sauce is the Boss!
Barbecue Sauce
FRANK'S RedHot ORIGINAL
TAMARI
REDUCED SODIUM
KOSHER SALT
Diamond Crystal
LA MORENA
Jalapeño Peppers
Chipotle Peppers
IN ADOBO SAUCE
Reddi wip
Original
SESAME TAHINI
Roland
Green Peppercorns
WHIRLY POP
HOT CHILI SAUCE
Kraft
Jet-Puffed
MARSHMALLOWS
Have fun with your yum!
HEINZ 57
TOMATO KETCHUP
HERSHEY'S

CRAFT BURGERS & CRAZY SHAKES

JOE ISIDORI

CRAFT & CRAZY

PHOTOGRAPHS BY MADONNA+CHILD

BURGERS

FROM

BLACK TAP

SHAKES

PAM KRAUSS BOOKS/AVERY
NEW YORK

an imprint of Penguin Random House LLC
375 Hudson Street
New York, New York 10014

ISBN 9780735215450

Printed in the United States of America

10 9 8 7 6 5 4 3 2 1

Book design by Madonna+Child

PUBLISHER'S NOTE

The recipes contained in this book are to be followed exactly as written. The publisher is not responsible for your specific health or allergy needs that may require medical supervision. The publisher is not responsible for any adverse reactions to the recipes contained in this book.

FOR MY FATHER,
ARTHUR

TODAY
ESPN APP

ACKNOWLEDGMENTS

The last couple of years have been full of great surprises for me, and being able to share the Black Tap experience with you as a book has been one of the best. I've been lucky to have help from many people, both with this project and with the restaurant that makes you want to read it. None of it would have happened without my mother; my stepfather, Don; my wife, Louise; my partner, Chris Barish, and every investor and staff member at Black Tap. Many thanks are due to them and also to:

Freddy Schoen-Kiewert
Anthony Giordiano
Chris and Julie Barish
Keith and Ann Barish
Bee Barish
Courtney Wright
Peter Caporal
Gustavo Ramirez
Bruce and Belina Buschel
Michael Schwartz
Shingo Inoue
Uncle Tommy and Aunt Cathy
Cathy Isidori
Tommy Isidori
Rosemarie Isidori
Grandma Jean
Grandma Fanny "Nanny"
The Beni Amino Family
The Isidori Family
The DeFeis Family
The Altese Family
Brian Gallarello
Alek Michaud
Pam Krauss and everyone at Pam Krauss Books
Meagan Camp
Melissa Moore
Raquel Pelzel
Evan Frost
Angela Salvatore
Anthony Nacci
Richie Akiva
Michael Goldberg
Khristina and Brian Eslick
Logan Eslick
Graeme Eslick
Sophia Eslick
Marc Pestore
Pat LaFrieda
Rose and Frank
Angelo and Lenny
Mike Abruzesse
Jimmy Merker
Ralph Pagano
Don Pintabona
Tony Shure
Adam Viento
Charlie Walk
Zaida Czarnecka
Brett Hansen
Steven DeVall
Richard Abate
The Gotham Burger Social Club
Our amazing digital influencer family
Jennifer Baum, Erica Schecter, Kay Lindsay, and the entire Bullfrog + Baum team

BLACK TAP
CRAFT BURGERS & BEER
TAKEOUT
BURGERS
BEER
EAT
HERE
OPEN

INTRODUCTION

Black Tap may be a modern restaurant born in the Instagram age, but we're all about nostalgia. Burgers and milkshakes are iconic American food, and the kind you love the best has a lot to do with how and where you enjoyed the ones you had as a kid and who you shared them with. For me, that was my dad.

My family is from the Belmont section of the Bronx, and I grew up watching my father and my grandmother cook in rough, tough restaurant kitchens. They taught me to make Italian-American classics like chicken Parmigiana and lasagna, and from a young age, I loved to try my hand at re-creating them—my way.

My father, Arthur Isidori, looked like a *Carlito's Way*–era Al Pacino with the sensibility of a charming Italian-American Anthony Bourdain. We didn't just cook together; I was his sidekick on eating tours all around New York City. We would get chow fun and pork dumplings at Wo Hop in Chinatown on Tuesday nights and hit Pasquale's Rigoletto on Arthur Avenue in the Bronx before a Yankees game for the best pork chops with vinegar peppers. But best of all, we liked to go to Piper's Kilt in Eastchester for a cheeseburger deluxe platter: a cheeseburger served with lettuce, tomato, pickle, and french fries. One plate, one price. That burger deluxe has become the model for what we do today at Black Tap: one plate with a burger and fries, always with lettuce, tomato, and pickle on the side. But the way we play with the formula at Black Tap, adding layers of flavor, textures, and a fine-dining sensibility, would probably baffle the crew at Piper's Kilt.

When I was growing up, my father always accused me of being too fancy. "It's never good enough for you!" he would say with a laugh. "You've got champagne tastes on a Budweiser budget." He was proud when the Culinary Institute of America (CIA) gave me a scholarship at nineteen, but also suspicious: He said, "I've been cooking for forty years and I know how to do things and what makes money. You don't need to go to a school to learn how to cook." He had five thriving red sauce joints in and around the city at the time I graduated and was bewildered when I didn't want to take over the family business. I respected his food, but I was ambitious, full of fine-dining aspirations, and determined to set out on my own.

I went to Miami to work for Chef Michael Schwartz at Nemo, a New American restaurant with multicultural influences. I had learned classic technique at the CIA and had a lot of confidence from growing up around my dad's kitchens but was still a bit of a bull in a china shop. Michael refined my technique and palate, and gave me an education about sourcing and creating sophisticated American food. He also introduced me to Shingo Inoue, the masterful sushi chef Michael hired when we opened Shoji Sushi. Watching and working with Shingo brought my skills to another level, and I give him all the credit when another chef watches me cook and says, "I didn't know you trained in Japan."

Black Tap might not seem like it has much in common with those cooking experiences, but if the luncheonette-style burgers and shakes we serve are maybe a bit more dramatic or modern, a little healthier, or even more delicious than the ones you remember, it's because they reflect what I've learned about how to source quality ingredients and how to handle them properly and balance their flavors.

My own style of cooking, though, really came into focus when I helped open Southfork Kitchen, a sustainable seafood and local ingredient restaurant that celebrated the East End of Long Island. Shortly after we opened, sadly, my father had a heart attack and died while working in his kitchen. After taking a few weeks off, I returned to Southfork on Christmas Eve. My sous-chef, Jimmy, who had been running the show in my absence, asked me if I was okay. "Not really," I told him, "but I'm gonna cook." And with that I started re-creating all my father's dishes, improvising with the ingredients on hand. I sent out lobster fra diavolo, fried sardines with salsa verde, and roasted salmon with anchovy caper sauce. In the middle of this whirlwind, Bruce, the owner, came busting into the kitchen:

"What are you doing? What's going on?"

"Don't screw with me today," I said. "I'm cooking my way."

"You don't understand," he shouted. "They love it!"

Channeling my father through my food that crazy night got me thinking about growing up in his kitchen and all the food adventures we'd had together. I love being creative in the kitchen and making people happy. It had always been my dream to do that in a fine restaurant. To be recognized for it with awards and to earn a Michelin star, a milestone I reached while working for the Trump organization creating restaurants for his hotel properties, was beyond my imagining. But when you cook in that kind of environment, you are pleasing a very small number of people—maybe 1 percent of the 1 percent. This New York City kid wanted to feed New York. And I wanted to have fun.

I started envisioning a neighborhood joint that would be a cross between a classic luncheonette or coffee shop and a corner bar. A place where we could flip some burgers, spin some shakes, and serve great beer. And in 2015 that dream became a reality when we opened Black Tap in the heart of SoHo. Black Tap reflects everything I've learned about food and business and sincerely reflects my own heritage and my desire to cook for the people, not just for me or for a privileged few.

The very first Black Tap on Broome Street looks like a dimly lit dive bar that's been there forever, a neighborhood secret with a cool, boisterous, friendly vibe. The menu, though, reflects my journey from New York City kid to Michelin-star chef and home again. On any given day, you'll find people in fashion, the arts, and business eating alongside construction workers on a lunch break, kids coming in at three p.m. from the school around the corner, and chefs unwinding over a beer after a long day.

This is the greatest food city in the world, and the busy people who live here have easy access to amazing meals, high and low, on every corner, sometimes more than one. It makes me proud that they keep returning to Black Tap when there are so many great burgers in this town, not to mention phenomenal tacos, ramen, spanakopita, and pastries right up the street.

I have never been prouder than the night

Coca-Cola

Special
Other

Black Tap won the People's Choice Award at the New York City Wine & Food Fest's 2015 Burger Bash. It's like winning an Oscar here in Burger World. When we decided to compete, everyone wanted me to make our classic All-American burger, but I wanted to do something extra special. We went in with our Greg Norman burger—Wagyu beef topped with blue cheese, arugula, and buttermilk sauce on a Martin's potato bun and we threw a party Black Tap style. Everyone from the restaurant was there—wearing hats, holding big signs, carrying trays, singing, chanting, and having fun. Bobby Flay was looking over at the sea of Black Tap hats bobbing in our corner of the roof and asked, "Who's the bozo who brought the circus with him?" When Rachael Ray announced us as the winner and gave me that trophy, it felt like a Babe Ruth moment.

From that day on, our burgers have been on the must-try list of every food tourist and burger-obsessed local in New York City. But we weren't done yet. I knew our menu needed one more element to fulfill my grown-up fantasy of re-creating that iconic luncheonette experience of my youth: shakes.

My dad and I had an eternal debate about what to drink with our burgers.

"I'm old school, I'll have an egg cream," my dad would announce. "You should have one, too."

"Pop, you know I like a milkshake," I'd protest.

"Ahh, you always have to be fancy."

Little did he know. Our crazy shakes have created a social media sensation, with millions of hits online and their very own Instagram hashtag. The restaurant is always jammed with visitors who want to taste them and post their own picture on Instagram. We have even had three-hour waits for milkshakes in the middle of a winter snowstorm! One visitor told me she felt like the shakes are very "New York": bold, big, colorful, and over-the-top. They're about a foot tall, and I get asked all the time if people actually finish them. The answer is yes, every day.

Bottom line: We're having fun at Black Tap. We want you to be happy when you eat here and I want you to have fun when you use this book to cook for your friends and family. Have a good time, and don't sweat the details too hard. If you follow a few simple rules, it's probably going to taste great. And if you enjoy yourself while you are cooking and sharing this food with people you care about, it's going to taste that much better.

mermaid pilsner
ACBC
EASY BLONDE
peak organic
BREWING COMPANY
Fresh Cut
Toasted Lager
BLUE POINT BREWING COMPANY
BROOKLYN LAGER
TECATE
ORIGINAL
BACK IN BLACK
BLACK DUCK
PORTER
GREENPORT HARBOR
OMMEGANG
WITTE WHEAT ALE
ANGRY ORCHARD
HARD CIDER
CRISP APPLE
Miller
HIGH LIFE
BRONX BREWERY
AMERICAN
PALE ALE
BENGALI

CRAFT BEER AT BLACK TAP

Craft beer is part of our DNA. We think about what we offer at the bar as carefully as we source and pair the high-quality ingredients we use in the kitchen. Today, great craft beers are being produced all over the world, but we like to keep it local. We work with many of the stellar breweries in our area, most notably Brooklyn Brewery, Six Point Brewery, and Bronx Brewery. If you're not in New York, though, no worries; craft beer production in the United States is exploding and it has never been easier to find a good local beer. But it can also be satisfying to go old school when pairing a beer with your burger. When I want to keep it real, my favorite beer of choice is an ice-cold Miller High Life.

CRAFT

BURGERS

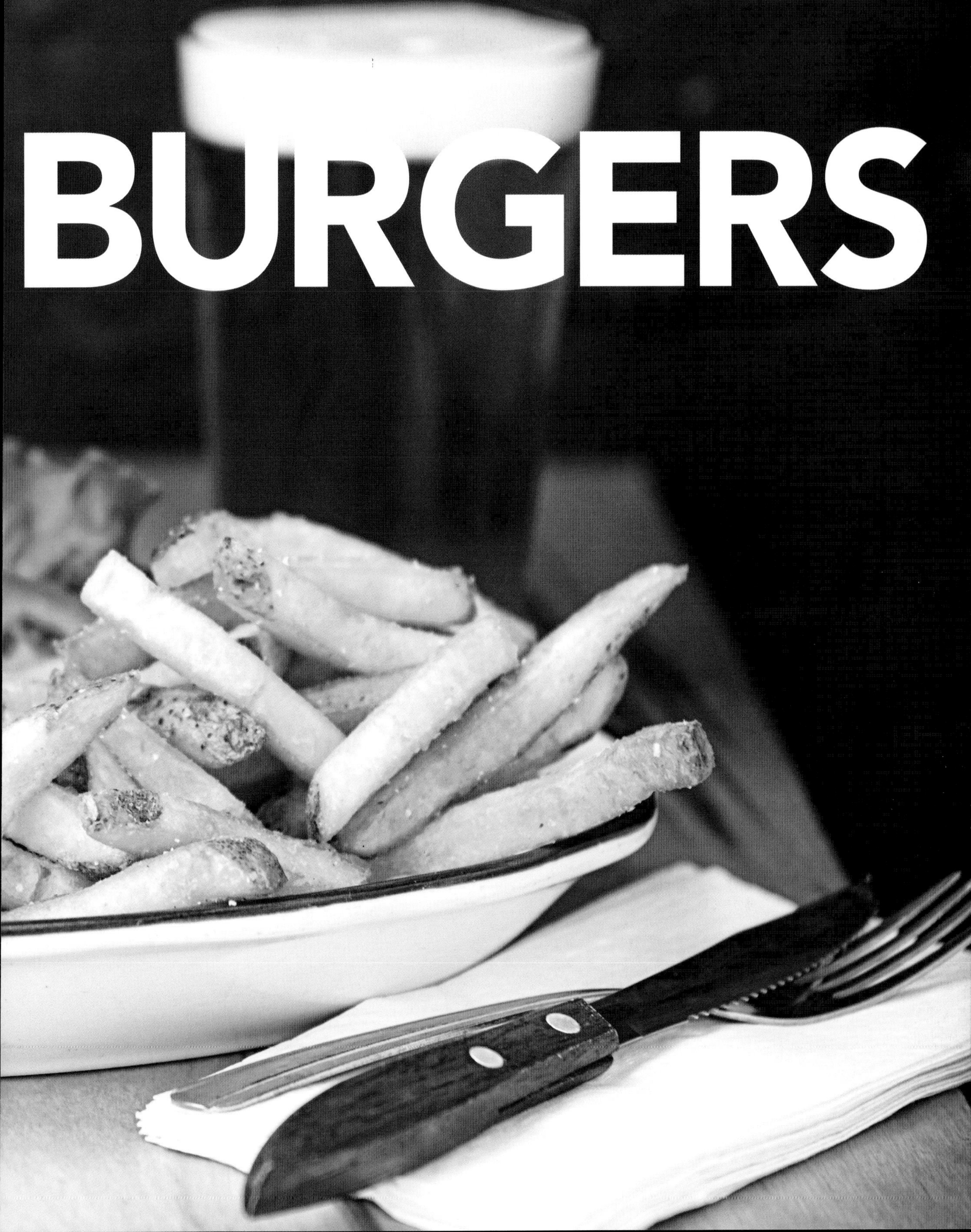

MAKING BURGERS, BLACK TAP STYLE

There are as many ways to make a burger as there are states in this country, and the one you like the best is probably the one you grew up eating. You can make a great one at home by paying attention to a few basics.

THE MEAT

When food is simple and straightforward, the quality of the components really matters, and a great burger starts with high-quality meat. At Black Tap, we use a mix of ground brisket and chuck. If you can't find brisket, ground short ribs would be a solid, if pricier, substitute. You can also make your burger from 100% ground chuck. Do not buy sirloin—it's too lean. Fat is your friend when you're making a hamburger. Fat makes a burger juicy and carries the flavor, so the higher the fat ratio in your meat, the juicier and more flavorful your burger is likely to be. Assuming you don't grind your own meat, ideally you want to go to the butcher and ask him to grind a mix to your specifications, grinding it as loosely as possible. If you buy your meat already ground at the grocery store, look for a package of ground brisket or chuck that has a ratio of at least 80 to 20 percent lean to fat. If you can find one that's 75/25, even better. And don't freeze it! For optimal texture and flavor, you want to use fresh meat. Save the frozen ground chuck for meat loaf.

80/20
GOOD,
75/25
BETTER

FLIP
ONCE

THE METHOD

When mixing and forming your burgers, handle the meat as minimally as possible to ensure a juicy, tender burger. When you divide the meat for patties, aim for something between a gut-busting monster burger and a super-thin burger: 6 to 8 ounces of beef is right for a classic diner patty. If you're using gamier meats, like bison or lamb, stay on the smaller side. Using a ring mold to shape the patties will keep your burgers a consistent size, but it's not a big deal if you don't have one; fold a long piece of foil into a 1-inch strip and form it into a collar. Tape the ends in place. Place the meat in the ring, if you are using one, using light pressure to create a perfectly even and not-too-thick patty. Otherwise, just pat the meat lightly into a patty with your open palms. Either way, don't pound it or roll it. When the meat is packed tightly, it takes longer to cook and will make a tougher burger. You're not making meatballs. Season the patties with kosher salt and cracked black pepper and leave them alone.

At Black Tap, the burgers are griddled, not grilled. At home, your best option is a cast-iron skillet or flat-top griddle, the older and more well seasoned the better. Cast iron retains heat like nothing else. Slick your cast-iron pan with just a touch of a neutral cooking oil and get it very hot before you add the patties. This is how you will create a nice crust on the burger and a juicy, soft interior. When the oil is shimmering, you can put the burger on. Once it hits the pan, don't touch it or move it except the one time you flip it to the second side. It will probably take three to four minutes on each side to reach a "chef's medium," which will give you a crusty brown sear with a pink juicy center. You will have a succulent burger that feels light and juicy in your mouth because you didn't overwork or overcook the meat. If there is a lot of rendered fat in the pan after you flip the burgers, carefully tip the pan and pour or spoon it out; otherwise, the burgers will steam rather than sear. Be sure to pour out most of the fat in the pan before you add the buns to toast them.

THE CHEESE

A great burger is about ratio, and I think one slice of cheese gets lost, so we almost always use two at Black Tap for that oozing, satisfying effect. Different burgers use different types of cheese, but American cheese is the burger classic for a reason: it tastes nostalgic and is made to melt. It's worth it to do a little steaming trick to melt the cheese like they do at a luncheonette. You'll need a lid to fit your pan and fast hands. When your burger is *just* done, put two slices of cheese on the burger, put a teaspoon of water in the pan to create steam, and cover the pan immediately. After about ten seconds (maybe a little longer if your pan is big) the cheese will be perfectly melted. It's critical to move decisively, because if you use too much water or steam for too long, it will change the texture of the burger or overcook it. Done correctly, this is the quickest way to give the cheese a nice gooey pull without changing the temperature of the meat.

USE
TWO
SLICES

MAKE IT SPECIAL

THE SAUCE

Every Black Tap burger is elevated and enhanced by one of our house-made sauces. A well-crafted sauce highlights the burger and adds a robust, spicy, or special note without smothering the flavor of the beef. Making them is worth your time. I think ketchup is for suckers or for french fries, but if you ask for it, I'm giving you Heinz. I like Heinz ketchup as an ingredient and a kind of mother sauce, but not on a burger.

THE BUN

You can get a burger on other things, like English muffins or brioche buns, but at Black Tap all our burgers are served on a Martin's potato bun. Its slightly sweet flavor profile is perfect for the diner-style burger you're making. It's soft, it's fluffy, and it toasts up nicely so the burger will not fall apart. For the best taste and texture, toast both top and bottom with a touch of butter or oil in a separate pan on your stovetop. If you don't have another pan, you can toast the bun in the same pan you used for the burgers, but make sure you drain out all but a tiny bit of the fat first; otherwise, it will be too greasy. Don't put your buns in the oven or the toaster—they'll dry out. A lot of home cooks overlook the ratio of meat to roll in the overall taste of their burger. You will not need to worry about this if you use the Martin's potato bun for a 6- to 8-ounce patty. We also have Udi's Gluten Free buns on hand at Black Tap for people who ask for them. They are a good alternative to Martin's potato buns.

THE SIDES

All our burgers come with the time-honored lunch-counter accompaniments: lettuce, tomato, and pickle. They are not an afterthought. Make sure yours are fresh and delicious enough to eat on their own. Just like a great burger is a careful balance of flavor, it's also about creating the right ratio of textures. The crispness of the lettuce and tomato or other toppings plays against the unctuous melted cheese and any other rich toppings, and their clean taste contrasts perfectly with the salt of the burger. We plate all our burgers with a kosher half-sour pickle on the side, because what is a New York burger without a kosher half-sour? No self-respecting New York deli or diner would send a plate out without one, and you shouldn't, either.

These rules are for Black Tap–style burgers. We understand what we are making, and we do not compromise. That should be your bottom line in the kitchen, too.

IF YOU MUST GRILL **I know for some of you, making burgers means grilling. Here's the problem: When you cook a piece of meat, you are looking for the Maillard reaction, the browning of protein that is the key to great flavor. It's not that you can't get that on a grill, but you need to understand the difference between a burger and other kinds of meat. A big, marbled rib-eye steak can form a nice crust on the grill without drying out because it takes long enough to cook. A burger does not require the same length of cooking, and the short time it needs to sear means it benefits from an even, controlled surface that a grill can't provide. If you are determined to cook on the grill, a cast-iron skillet or griddle on top of the grill grates will give you a nice, even crust and char with a tender interior. Close the lid of your grill over the pan or griddle to get it really hot, and prime the surface before you cook the burgers, just like you would if you were cooking on the stovetop. If you really want the grill marks and smoky flavor cooking over an open flame adds, I think you need to baste the burger constantly with barbecue sauce, which may get you a burger you like, but it will not be Black Tap style or rooted in the classic luncheonette burger experience.**

NY

♥

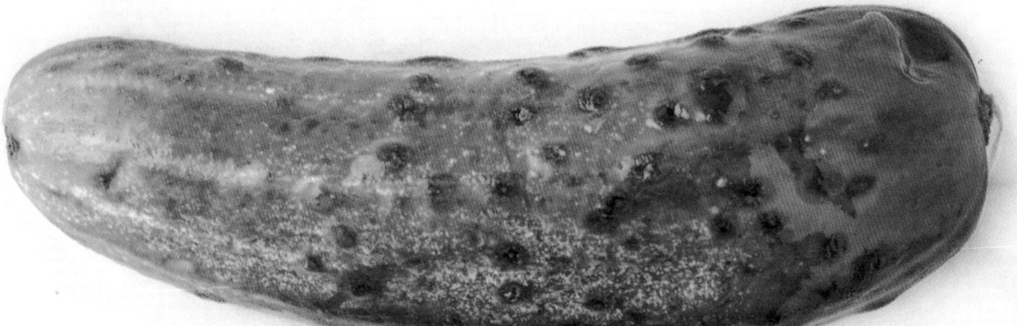

Martin's
4 Inch
FAMOUS Dutch TASTE
POTATO ROLLS
RESTAURANT PACK
NOT FOR RESALE
K DAIRY
25.5 OZ. (1 LB 9.5 OZ.) 723 GRAMS
HEINZ 57 VARIETIES
HEINZ
ESTD 1869 ESTD
TOMATO KETCHUP
57 VARIETIES
GROWN NOT MADE
NET WT 14 OZ (397g)
HOT PEPPER PASTE
NET WT. 1.1 lb (500g)
500g
Gold MEDAL
ALL-PURPOSE
Deliciously Smooth Every Time

BURGER/SALADS/SAUCES/SIDES GROCERY LIST

- Martin's potato buns
- Pat LaFrieda beef
- Sweet Baby Ray's BBQ Sauce
- Heinz ketchup
- Gulden's spicy brown mustard
- Maille Dijon mustard
- Kosher half-sour pickles
- Shaoxing cooking wine
- La Morena chipotle in adobo
- La Morena pickled jalapeños
- Diamond Crystal kosher salt
- Wondra flour
- Frank's Red Hot sauce
- Valentina hot sauce
- Sriracha
- Kimchi base
- Tahini
- Gochujang (Korean pepper paste)
- Kadoya toasted sesame oil
- San-J Gluten-Free Tamari
- Roland green peppercorns in brine
- Urbani black truffle oil
- Canned and/or dried garbanzo beans
- Japanese yuzu juice
- Toasted white sesame seeds
- San Marzano double-concentrated tomato paste
- Sclafani crushed tomatoes

DELUXE

ALL-AMERICAN BURGER

SERVES 4

This is it: the classic, the inspiration, and the burger I usually suggest people order if they are new to Black Tap. It's based on the basic cheeseburger deluxe on the menu of every New York diner of my childhood—it's griddled, never grilled, to medium, topped with two slices of American cheese and served on a Martin's potato bun with lettuce, tomato, and raw onion (if you want it), all on a single plate with a side of french fries and a pickle.

BEST BEER: MILLER HIGH LIFE

2 POUNDS 80% LEAN GROUND BEEF

1½ TABLESPOONS KOSHER SALT

½ TEASPOON FRESHLY GROUND BLACK PEPPER

CANOLA OR VEGETABLE OIL FOR THE PAN

8 SLICES AMERICAN CHEESE

FOUR 4-INCH POTATO BUNS

4 TABLESPOONS SPECIAL SAUCE (page 66)

TOMATO SLICES, LETTUCE, PICKLE SPEARS, FOR SERVING

1 Place the ground beef in a large bowl and gently use your fingers to fluff the meat to loosen it. Use a 5-inch metal ring or your hands to make four ¾-inch-thick patties. Mix the salt and pepper together in a small bowl and use half of it to generously season the tops of the burger patties.

2 Heat a cast-iron flat-top griddle or large cast-iron skillet over medium-high heat for 2 minutes. Dip a folded paper towel in oil and use it to grease the pan. With a spatula, carefully transfer the patties to the pan, seasoned-side down. Sprinkle the patties with the remaining salt and pepper mixture. Cook, without pressing down or moving the burgers, until the bottoms are browned, about 5 minutes. Flip the burgers over and continue to cook for 4½ to 5 minutes longer for medium-rare or 7 minutes for medium. If necessary, spoon out the excess fat from the pan. Place 2 slices of the cheese on each patty, add 1 teaspoon water to the pan, and cover the pan immediately. Cook for 10 seconds (or a few seconds longer, if your pan is large), until the cheese has melted, then transfer the burgers to a plate.

3 Pour off most of the fat from the pan and use a paper towel to wipe out the browned bits. Open the buns and place the bottom halves cut-side down in the hot pan until browned and toasted, 1 to 2 minutes. Turn the buns over to toast the other side, 30 seconds to 1 minute longer. Repeat with the bun tops.

4 Transfer each patty to a bottom bun half. Smear each bun top with 1 tablespoon of the Special Sauce. Add a tomato slice to the top of the burger and cover with lettuce, then place the top bun half on the burger and serve with a pickle.

CALIFORNIA BURGER

SERVES 4

We call this the Perfect Ten. The Californian is the bestselling burger at Black Tap after the All-American. Turkey burgers are a leaner choice than beef but they can also be less flavorful and dry. Ours is a mixture of white and dark turkey meat, which makes it juicier than most, and we season it with an amazing mix that people can't always identify. Now you have the secret: it's Chinese five-spice, chili powder, and madras curry powder. This gets a cool, creamy touch from avocado, Swiss cheese, and a swipe of truffle mayo.

BEST BEER: WITTE WHEAT ALE, BREWERY OMMEGANG, COOPERSTOWN, NEW YORK

1 POUND GROUND WHITE-MEAT TURKEY
1 POUND GROUND DARK-MEAT TURKEY
¼ TEASPOON CHINESE FIVE-SPICE POWDER
¼ TEASPOON MADRAS CURRY POWDER
1 TABLESPOON KOSHER SALT
¼ TEASPOON FRESHLY GROUND BLACK PEPPER
CANOLA OR VEGETABLE OIL FOR THE PAN
8 SLICES SWISS CHEESE
FOUR 4-INCH POTATO BUNS
4 TABLESPOONS BLACK TRUFFLE MAYO (page 51)
1 HASS AVOCADO, SLICED
½ CUP PICKLED RED ONIONS (page 72)
LETTUCE, TOMATO SLICES, PICKLE SPEARS, FOR SERVING

1 Place all the ground turkey in a large bowl and gently use your fingers to fluff the meat to loosen it. Add the Chinese five-spice powder and curry powder and mix to combine, blending the light and dark meat together as best as you can (you don't want to overhandle the meat). Use a 4½- to 5-inch metal ring or your hands to form four ¾-inch-thick patties. Mix the salt and pepper together in a small bowl and use half of it to season the tops of the patties.

2 Heat a cast-iron flat-top griddle or large cast-iron skillet over medium-high heat for 2 minutes. Dip a folded paper towel in oil and use it to grease the pan. Use a spatula to transfer the patties carefully to the pan, seasoned-side down. Season the tops of the burgers with the remaining salt and pepper and cook, without pressing down on the burgers, until both sides are browned and the internal temperature of a patty registers 165°F on an instant-read thermometer, 12 to 14 minutes total, turning the burgers midway through cooking. Place 2 slices of cheese on each burger, add 1 teaspoon water to the pan, and cover the pan immediately. Cook for 10 seconds, until the cheese has melted. Transfer the burgers to a plate.

3 Wipe out the pan to remove any browned bits and most of the rendered fat. Open the buns and place the bottom halves cut-side down in the hot pan until browned and toasted, 1 to 2 minutes. Turn the buns over to toast the other side, 30 seconds to 1 minute longer. Repeat with the bun tops.

4 Transfer each patty to a bottom bun half. Spread the bun with 1 tablespoon of the Black Truffle Mayo. Top with one-quarter of the avocado slices and pickled red onions. Place the bun on the burger and serve with the lettuce, tomato slice, and pickle on the side.

BISTRO
style

STEAK AU POIVRE BURGER

SERVES 4

The year we opened, Zagat called this one of the best new burgers in New York. It's an unctuous play on the steakhouse classic and the traditional flavors of French cuisine. The green peppercorn sauce is made with a touch of cream and brandy to highlight the beef; you'll have about ½ cup left over, so try it with your next steak dinner, too. The Steak au Poivre Burger is great with fries, just like its original bistro inspiration, but we especially love it with onion rings.

BEST BEER: BACK IN BLACK IPA, 21ST AMENDMENT BREWERY, SAN FRANCISCO, CALIFORNIA

Green Peppercorn Sauce

1½ TABLESPOONS UNSALTED BUTTER (1 TABLESPOON AT ROOM TEMPERATURE)

½ MEDIUM SPANISH ONION, FINELY CHOPPED

2 TABLESPOONS DRAINED GREEN PEPPERCORNS IN BRINE

2 TABLESPOONS SHAOXING COOKING WINE

½ CUP HEAVY CREAM

1 TEASPOON APPLE CIDER VINEGAR

1 TEASPOON WORCESTERSHIRE SAUCE

1 TEASPOON KITCHEN BOUQUET OR GRAVY MASTER

¼ CUP CRUMBLED BLUE CHEESE

Burgers

2 POUNDS 80% LEAN GROUND BEEF

1 TABLESPOON KOSHER SALT

¼ TEASPOON FRESHLY GROUND BLACK PEPPER

CANOLA OR VEGETABLE OIL FOR THE PAN

½ CUP CRUMBLED BLUE CHEESE

FOUR 4-INCH POTATO BUNS

LETTUCE, TOMATO SLICES, PICKLE SPEARS, FOR SERVING

1 Melt the ½ tablespoon of cold butter in a medium saucepan over medium heat. Add the onion and cook, stirring often, until browned, 8 to 10 minutes. Stir in the green peppercorns and cook for 1 minute, then pour in the cooking wine and cook, stirring often, until half the liquid has evaporated, about 1 minute. Stir in the cream, vinegar, Worcestershire, and Kitchen Bouquet. Reduce the heat to low and cook, stirring often, until the liquid has reduced by half, about 5 minutes.

2 Turn off the heat and set the sauce aside to cool for 10 minutes, then pour it into a blender. Add the cheese and the remaining 1 tablespoon butter with the motor running and blend until the sauce is smooth, about 30 seconds. Transfer to a small saucepan and set aside. The sauce can also be refrigerated in an airtight container for up to 1 week.

3 Place the ground beef in a large bowl and gently use your fingers to fluff the meat to loosen it (you don't want to overhandle the meat). Use a 4½- to 5-inch metal ring or your hands to make four ¾-inch-thick patties. Mix the salt and pepper together in a small bowl and use half of it to season the tops of the burger generously.

4 Heat a cast-iron flat-top griddle or large cast-iron skillet over medium-high heat for 2 minutes. Dip a folded paper towel in oil and use it to grease the pan. Use a spatula to carefully transfer the patties to the pan, seasoned-side down. Sprinkle the patties with the remaining salt and pepper mixture. Cook without pressing down or moving the burgers until the bottoms are browned, about 5 minutes. Flip the burgers over and continue to cook for 4½ to 5 minutes longer for medium-rare or 7 minutes more for medium. Sprinkle each burger with 2 tablespoons of the blue cheese, then cover the pan until the cheese has melted, about 1 minute. Transfer the burgers to a plate.

5 Pour off most of the fat from the pan and use a paper towel to wipe out the browned bits. Open the buns and place the bottom halves cut-side down in the hot pan until browned and toasted, 1 to 2 minutes. Turn the buns over to toast the other side, 30 seconds to 1 minute longer. Repeat with the bun tops.

6 Transfer each patty to a bottom bun half and cover with the top bun. Warm the sauce over medium heat, stirring so it doesn't burn. Serve the burgers with lettuce, a tomato slice, and a pickle spear, with the Green Peppercorn Sauce on the side.

SPICY MEXICAN BURGER

SERVES 4

Whip up this big, bold pork burger if you're also in the mood for a taco. At Black Tap, we use a blend of ground pork and traditional spices similar to the fresh chorizo from the butcher case. Let it cure overnight if you can; it will hold together better. Pepper Jack cheese and Chipotle Mayo complement and cool the spicy chorizo. Zagat called it one of the 12 Best New Burgers in New York.

BEST BEER: FRESH CUT PILSNER, PEAK ORGANIC BREWING COMPANY, PORTLAND, MAINE

---

3 DRIED GUAJILLO CHILES
1 ROUNDED TABLESPOON RED PEPPER FLAKES
⅔ CUP APPLE CIDER VINEGAR
2 TABLESPOONS SWEET PAPRIKA
1 TABLESPOON PLUS ¼ TEASPOON CHILI POWDER
1½ TEASPOONS GARLIC POWDER
1¾ TEASPOONS FRESHLY GROUND BLACK PEPPER
1½ TEASPOONS ONION POWDER
¾ TEASPOON GROUND CORIANDER
¾ TEASPOON FRESHLY GRATED NUTMEG
1 TEASPOON DRIED OREGANO
¾ TEASPOON GROUND CUMIN
1 MEDIUM GARLIC CLOVE
1½ TABLESPOONS KOSHER SALT
1½ POUNDS GROUND PORK
CANOLA OR VEGETABLE OIL FOR THE PAN
8 SLICES PEPPER JACK CHEESE
FOUR 4-INCH POTATO BUNS
¼ CUP PICO DE GALLO (page 66)
CHIPOTLE MAYO (page 44)
LETTUCE, TOMATO SLICES, PICKLE SPEARS, AND LIME WEDGES FOR SERVING

1 Coarsely tear up the chiles, discarding the seeds and stems, and place them in a medium bowl with the red pepper flakes. Cover with the vinegar and set aside for 1 hour to soften.

2 Add the paprika, chili powder, garlic powder, 1½ teaspoons of the black pepper, the onion powder, coriander, nutmeg, oregano, and cumin to a medium skillet and toast over medium heat, stirring often, until the spices are fragrant, about 1 minute. Transfer to a plate to cool.

3 Place the guajillo-vinegar mixture, garlic, and ½ tablespoon of the salt in a blender and blend until smooth, 30 seconds to 1 minute.

4 Put the pork in a large bowl and add the guajillo sauce and the toasted spices. Work the meat and seasonings together with your hands until just combined (you don't want to overhandle the meat). Transfer the chorizo mixture to an airtight container and refrigerate for at least 24 hours and preferably up to 2 days.

5 Use a 4½- to 5-inch metal ring or your hands to form four ¾-inch-thick patties. Mix the remaining 1 tablespoon salt and ¼ teaspoon black pepper together in a small bowl and use half of it to generously season the tops of the burger patties.

6 Heat a cast-iron flat-top griddle or large cast-iron skillet over medium-high heat for 2 minutes. Dip a folded paper towel in oil and use it to grease the pan. With a spatula, carefully transfer the patties to the pan, seasoned-side down. Sprinkle the patties with the remaining salt and pepper mixture. Cook, without pressing down or moving the burgers, until the bottoms are browned, 4 to 5 minutes. Flip the burgers and cook until an instant-read thermometer registers 145°F, 4 to 5 minutes longer. Place 2 slices of cheese on each burger, add 1 teaspoon water to the pan, and cover the pan immediately. Cook until the cheese has melted, about 10 seconds, then transfer the burgers to a plate.

7 Pour off most of the fat from the pan and use a paper towel to wipe out the browned bits. Open the buns and place the bottom halves cut-side down in the hot pan until browned and toasted, 1 to 2 minutes. Turn the buns over to toast the other side, 30 seconds to 1 minute longer. Repeat with the bun tops.

8 Transfer each patty to a bottom bun half. Top with Pico de Gallo. Spread the Chipotle Mayo on the top bun half. Serve with lettuce, a tomato slice, pickle, and lime wedge, to enhance the flavor of the chorizo.

PICO DE GALLO

GRASS-FED

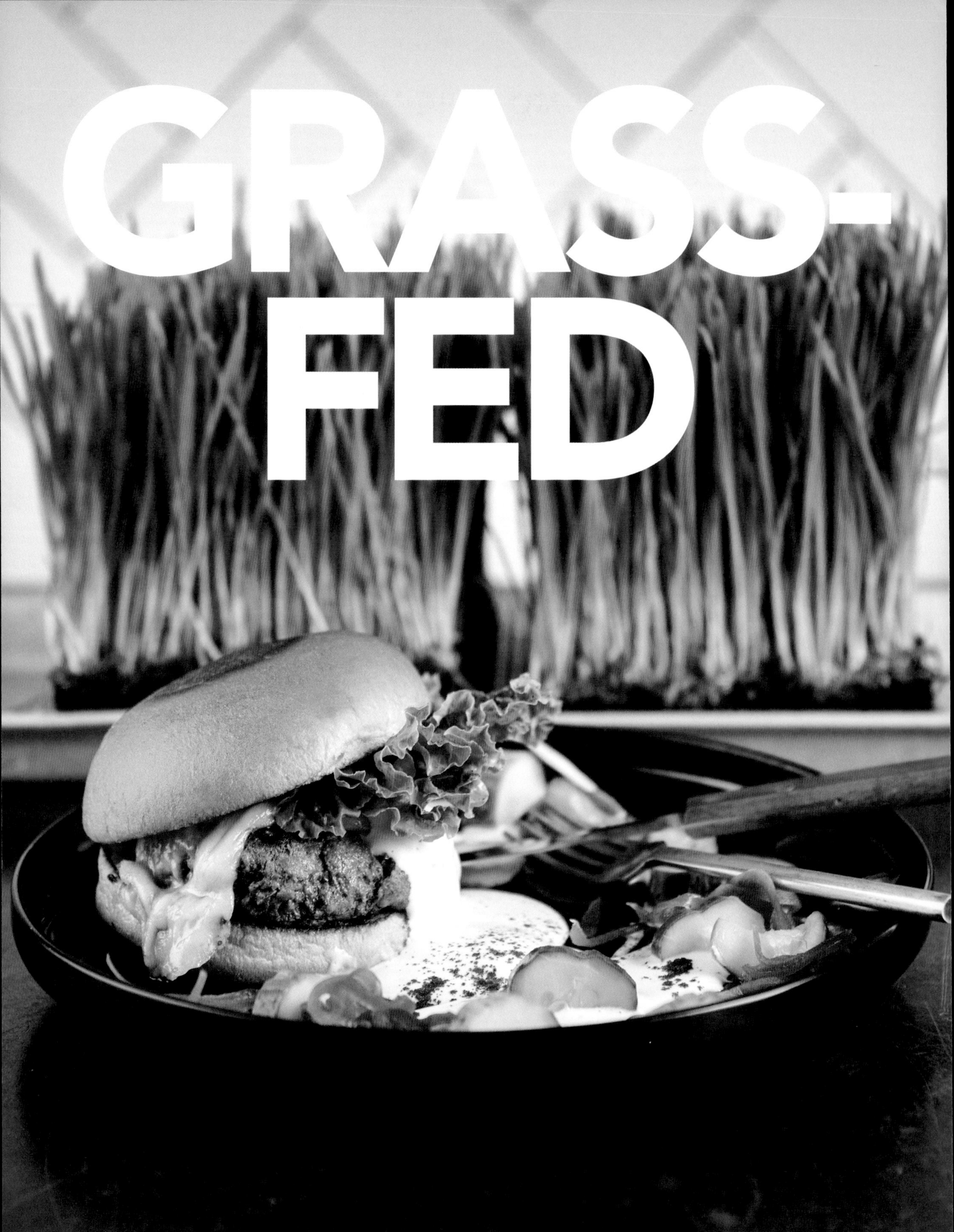

LAMB BURGER

SERVES 4

This burger, which we make with local grass-fed lamb, is our Greek-American diner play, because many people associate lamb with Greece, where it is so popular. Lamb makes a funky alternative to a beef burger, and its richness is nicely balanced by Swiss cheese, tangy homemade pickled onions, crunchy fresh cucumber, and our Buttermilk-Dill Dressing. It's a burger that manages to be comforting and sophisticated at the same time. It tastes best if you keep it medium-rare.

BEST BEER: AMERICAN PALE ALE, BRONX BREWERY, BRONX, NEW YORK

1½ POUNDS GROUND LAMB

1 TABLESPOON KOSHER SALT

¼ TEASPOON FRESHLY GROUND BLACK PEPPER

CANOLA OR VEGETABLE OIL FOR THE PAN

8 SLICES SWISS CHEESE

FOUR 4-INCH POTATO BUNS

2 HALF-SOUR PICKLES, SLICED CROSSWISE INTO ROUNDS

½ CUP DRAINED PICKLED RED ONIONS (page 72)

LETTUCE, TOMATO SLICES, PICKLE SPEARS, FOR SERVING

1 CUP BUTTERMILK-DILL DRESSING (page 66)

1 Place the lamb in a large bowl and gently use your fingers to fluff it to loosen the meat (you don't want to overhandle the meat). Use a 4- to 4½-inch metal ring or your hands to form four ¾-inch-thick patties. Mix the salt and pepper together in a small bowl and use half of it to generously season the tops of the burger patties.

2 Heat a cast-iron flat-top griddle or large cast-iron skillet over medium-high heat for 2 minutes. Dip a folded paper towel in oil and use it to grease the pan. With a spatula, carefully transfer the patties to the pan, seasoned-side down. Sprinkle the patties with the remaining salt and pepper mixture. Cook, without pressing down or moving the burgers, until the bottoms are browned, 4 to 5 minutes. Flip the burgers and cook until both sides are browned, 9 to 10 minutes for medium-rare and 12 minutes for medium. Place 2 slices of cheese on each burger, add 1 teaspoon water to the pan, and cover the pan immediately. Cook just until the cheese has melted, about 10 seconds. Transfer the burgers to a plate.

3 Pour off most of the fat from the pan and use a paper towel to wipe out the browned bits. Open the buns and place the bottom halves cut-side down in the hot pan until browned and toasted, 1 to 2 minutes. Turn the buns over to toast the other side, about 1 minute longer. Repeat with the bun tops.

4 Transfer each patty to a bottom bun half. Top with pickle slices and pickled onions and serve with lettuce, a tomato slice, and a pickle spear, with the Buttermilk-Dill Dressing on the side.

FALAFEL BURGER

SERVES 4

I'll be honest—I find most veggie burgers bland and mushy, so I struggled when I was considering a vegetarian offering for Black Tap. This falafel, which is based on a recipe I developed with Michael Schwartz in Miami, was the solution. It's more of a Parisian- or Israeli-style falafel that reverses the ratio of herbs to chickpeas you find in many recipes. All the parsley, cilantro, and mint create a vibrant, herbaceous flavor that is complemented by homemade tahini, hummus, pickled onions, and feta cheese. We make these fresh every morning, flash-fry them, and sell out every day. At home, you'll probably find it easier to panfry them in a skillet, rather than deep-frying them.

BEST BEER: ANGRY ORCHARD HARD APPLE CIDER (GREAT IF YOU WANT TO STAY GLUTEN-FREE)

½ POUND DRIED CHICKPEAS

½ SMALL RED ONION, QUARTERED

¾ CUP LIGHTLY PACKED FRESH FLAT-LEAF PARSLEY LEAVES

¾ CUP LIGHTLY PACKED FRESH CILANTRO LEAVES

½ CUP FRESH MINT LEAVES

1½ TEASPOONS GROUND CUMIN

1½ TEASPOONS BAKING POWDER

1½ TEASPOONS KOSHER SALT

1 CUP CANOLA OR VEGETABLE OIL, FOR FRYING

FOUR 4-INCH POTATO BUNS

½ CUP CRUMBLED FETA CHEESE

¼ CUP DRAINED PICKLED RED ONIONS (page 72)

1 CUP HUMMUS (page 67)

LETTUCE, TOMATO SLICES, PICKLE SPEARS, FOR SERVING

¾ CUP TAHINI SAUCE (page 63)

1 Place the chickpeas in a large bowl and add room-temperature water to cover them by 2 inches. Set the chickpeas aside to soak overnight.

2 The next day, drain the chickpeas and place them in a food processor. Add the onion, parsley, cilantro, mint, cumin, baking powder, and salt and pulse three or four times to break up the ingredients. Process until the mixture is well combined and holds together when squeezed in your palm, 45 seconds to 1 minute.

3 Use a 4- to 4½-inch metal ring or your hands to make four ¾-inch-thick patties.

4 Pour the oil into a large, deep skillet and heat it over high heat for 1½ minutes. Working in batches, add the falafel patties to the pan (avoid overcrowding the pan) and cook until deeply browned and crispy on both sides, 8 to 10 minutes, turning the patties midway through the cooking time. Transfer the patties to a paper towel–lined plate to drain.

5 Heat a cast-iron flat-top griddle or large cast-iron skillet over medium-high heat for 2 minutes. Open the buns and place the bottom halves cut-side down in the hot pan until browned and toasted, 1 to 2 minutes. Turn the buns over to toast the other side, about 1 minute longer. Repeat with the bun tops.

6 Place each falafel patty on a bottom bun half. Top with feta cheese and pickled onions. Spread each bun top with ¼ cup of the Hummus and set them on top of the burgers. Serve with lettuce, a tomato slice, and a pickle spear, with the Tahini Sauce on the side.

HERBA-LICIOUS

OH
BABY!

TEXAN BURGER

SERVES 4

Chain restaurants were not a big thing for me growing up in New York, which is full of mom-and-pop places, neighborhood joints, and trattorias. I got my real fast-food education when I was spending more time out west, working for the Trump Organization. Carl's Jr.'s Western burger was one of my favorites. It's essentially a barbecue bacon cheeseburger, and so is the Texan. People call it our Big Boy Burger. It's topped with bacon and aged cheddar, BBQ sauce, and mayo, and has an incredible umami factor. A homemade onion ring gives crunch to this burger, and also makes a perfect side.

BEST BEER: BENGALI IPA, SIXPOINT BREWERY, BROOKLYN, NEW YORK

---

2 POUNDS 80% LEAN GROUND BEEF

1 TABLESPOON KOSHER SALT

⅛ TEASPOON FRESHLY GROUND BLACK PEPPER

CANOLA OR VEGETABLE OIL FOR THE PAN

½ CUP CAROLINA-STYLE BBQ SAUCE (page 47) **OR YOUR FAVORITE STORE-BOUGHT SAUCE**

8 SLICES CHEDDAR CHEESE

FOUR 4-INCH POTATO BUNS

8 SLICES APPLEWOOD-SMOKED BACON, COOKED CRISP

8 ONION RINGS (page 71)

¼ CUP MAYONNAISE

LETTUCE, TOMATO SLICES, PICKLE SPEARS, FOR SERVING

1 Place the ground beef in a large bowl and gently use your fingers to fluff the meat to loosen it (you don't want to overhandle the meat). Use a 4½- to 5-inch metal ring or your hands to make four ¾-inch-thick patties. Mix the salt and pepper together in a small bowl and use half of it to generously season the tops of the burger patties.

2 Heat a cast-iron flat-top griddle or large cast-iron skillet over medium-high heat for 2 minutes. Dip a folded paper towel in oil and use it to grease the pan. Use a spatula to carefully transfer the patties to the pan and place them seasoned-side down. Sprinkle the tops of the patties with the remaining salt and pepper mixture. Cook, without pressing down or moving the burgers, until the bottoms are browned, about 5 minutes. Flip the burgers and cook for 4½ to 5 minutes longer for medium-rare or 7 minutes more for medium. Spoon 2 tablespoons of the barbecue sauce onto each burger, top with 2 slices of the cheese, and add 1 teaspoon water to the pan. Immediately cover the pan and cook until the cheese has melted, about 10 seconds. Transfer the burgers to a plate.

3 Pour off most of the fat from the pan and use a paper towel to wipe out the browned bits. Open the buns and place the bottom halves cut-side down in the hot pan until browned and toasted, 1 to 2 minutes. Turn the buns over to toast the other side, 30 seconds to 1 minute longer. Repeat with the bun tops.

4 Transfer each patty to a bottom bun half. Top each with 2 slices of the bacon and 2 onion rings. Spread mayonnaise on the top bun half. Serve with the lettuce, a tomato slice, and a pickle on the side.

BISON BURGER

SERVES 4

These day, people want to eat healthier, and we're conscientious about making sure Black Tap has something for everyone. Grass-fed bison is relatively low in cholesterol, fat, and calories and tastes satisfyingly beefy and tender, even though it's lean. We pair it with cold fresh mozzarella, lightly dressed arugula, roasted tomatoes, and a bit of pesto mayo. When we put this sophisticated, alternative burger on the menu, I figured it would be a bit of a specialty item, but it was wildly popular from the start, and it turns out that even kids love it. If you have been avoiding burgers because of concerns about your health or your waistline, give this recipe a try. If you don't have time to make the roasted tomatoes, you can often find them in jars near the antipasto items in your grocery store.

BEST BEER: ALPHABET CITY BREWING COMPANY EASY BLONDE ALE, NEW YORK, NEW YORK

Roasted Tomatoes

8 PLUM TOMATOES, STEM ENDS TRIMMED

2 TEASPOONS OLIVE OIL

KOSHER SALT AND FRESHLY GROUND BLACK PEPPER

Chimichurri Mayo

¼ CUP MAYONNAISE

1 TABLESPOON CHIMICHURRI SAUCE (page 59)

Burgers

1½ POUNDS GROUND BISON

1½ TABLESPOONS KOSHER SALT

½ TEASPOON FRESHLY GROUND BLACK PEPPER

CANOLA OR VEGETABLE OIL FOR THE PAN

FOUR 4-INCH POTATO BUNS

4 SLICES FRESH MOZZARELLA CHEESE

2 CUPS BABY ARUGULA

4 OUNCES PARMIGIANO-REGGIANO CHEESE, GRATED ON A MICROPLANE-STYLE RASP

LETTUCE, TOMATO SLICES, PICKLE SPEARS, FOR SERVING

1 Preheat the oven to 250°F. Arrange the tomatoes on a rimmed baking sheet and drizzle with the olive oil. Roast until the tomatoes are very soft and have collapsed, about 90 minutes. Let cool, then slip off the skins. Sprinkle with salt and pepper. (You can refrigerate the roasted tomatoes for several days, so feel free to double the recipe.)

2 Stir the mayonnaise and Chimichurri Sauce together in a small bowl, cover with plastic wrap, and refrigerate until ready to use. (The Chimichurri Mayo keeps in an airtight container in the refrigerator for up to 5 days.)

3 Place the bison in a large bowl and gently use your fingers to fluff the meat to loosen it (you don't want to overhandle the meat). Use a 6-inch metal ring or your hands to make four ½- to ¾-inch-thick patties. Carefully remove the ring and repeat with the remaining meat to make 4 patties. Mix the salt and pepper together in a small bowl and use it to season both sides of the burger patties.

4 Heat a cast-iron flat-top griddle or large cast-iron skillet over medium-high heat for 2 minutes. Dip a folded paper towel in oil and use it to grease the pan. With a spatula, carefully transfer the patties to the pan and cook until both sides are browned, 9 to 10 minutes for medium-rare and 12 minutes for medium, turning the burgers midway through the cooking time. Transfer the burgers to a plate.

5 Pour off most of the fat from the pan and use a paper towel to wipe out the browned bits. Open the buns and place the bottom halves cut-side down in the hot pan until browned and toasted, 1 to 2 minutes. Turn the buns over to toast the other side, about 1 minute longer. Repeat with the bun tops.

6 Transfer each patty to a bottom bun half. Top each burger with a slice of mozzarella, 2 roasted tomatoes, ½ cup of the baby arugula, and the grated cheese. Spread the bun tops with the Chimichurri Mayo and place them on the burgers. Serve with lettuce, a tomato slice, and a pickle on the side.

HEALTHY (ISH)

OLD TIMEY

OLD-FASHIONED BURGER

SERVES 4

This is the Black Tap tribute to the first hamburger sandwich, the kind made of chopped meat with grilled onions on toasted white bread you can still get at Louis' Lunch in New Haven. It also has elements of a New York diner patty melt, which is a burger with white cheese, onions, and mushrooms, maybe served on rye toast or an English muffin. Our homage to Old New York uses caramelized onions, sautéed mushrooms, and horseradish sauce to make a comforting burger that more than one customer has said reminds them of their childhood.

BEST BEER: BLUE POINT BREWING CO., LONG ISLAND, NEW YORK

1 TABLESPOON EXTRA-VIRGIN OLIVE OIL

1 TABLESPOON UNSALTED BUTTER

1 SMALL YELLOW ONION, FINELY CHOPPED

6 OUNCES SLICED WHITE BUTTON MUSHROOM CAPS (ABOUT 4 CUPS)

1 TABLESPOON PLUS 1 TEASPOON KOSHER SALT

½ TEASPOON FRESHLY GROUND BLACK PEPPER

2 POUNDS 80% LEAN GROUND BEEF

CANOLA OR VEGETABLE OIL FOR THE PAN

8 SLICES SWISS CHEESE

FOUR 4-INCH POTATO BUNS

½ CUP STORE-BOUGHT HORSERADISH SAUCE

LETTUCE, TOMATO SLICES, PICKLE SPEARS, FOR SERVING

1 Heat a medium skillet over medium-high heat. Add the olive oil and butter. Once the butter has melted, add the onion and cook, stirring often, until it is tender and translucent, 3 to 4 minutes. Add the mushrooms, 1 teaspoon of the salt, and ¼ teaspoon of the pepper and cook, stirring often, until the liquid released by the mushrooms has cooked off and the mushrooms are tender, about 5 minutes. Transfer the onion-mushroom mixture to a medium bowl and set aside.

2 Place the ground beef in a large bowl and gently use your fingers to fluff the meat to loosen it (you don't want to overhandle the meat). Use a 4½- to 5-inch metal ring or your hands to make four ¾-inch-thick patties. Mix the remaining 1 tablespoon salt and remaining ¼ teaspoon pepper together in a small bowl and use half of it to generously season the tops of the burger patties.

3 Heat a cast-iron flat-top griddle or large cast-iron skillet over medium-high heat for 2 minutes. Dip a folded paper towel in oil and use it to grease the pan. Use a spatula to carefully transfer the patties to the pan and place them seasoned-side down. Sprinkle the patties with the remaining salt and pepper mixture. Cook, without pressing down or moving the burgers, until the bottoms are browned, about 5 minutes. Flip the burgers and cook for 4½ to 5 minutes longer for medium-rare or 7 minutes more for medium. Place 2 slices of cheese on each patty, add 1 teaspoon water to the pan, and cover the pan immediately. Cook for 10 seconds (or a few seconds longer, if your pan is large), until the cheese has melted, then transfer the burgers to a plate.

4 Pour out most of the fat from the pan and use a paper towel to wipe out the browned bits. Open the buns and place the bottom halves cut-side down in the hot pan until browned and toasted, 1 to 2 minutes. Turn the buns over to toast the other side, 30 seconds to 1 minute longer. Repeat with the bun tops.

5 Transfer each patty to a bottom bun half. Top each patty with some of the onion-mushroom mixture. Smear 2 tablespoons of horseradish sauce onto each bun half. Serve with lettuce, a tomato slice, and a pickle on the side.

PIZZA BURGER

SERVES 4 (WITH 3 CUPS LEFTOVER SAUCE FOR YOUR NEXT PASTA DINNER)

Most people count pizza and burgers among their favorite foods, so it was no surprise that this was an immediate hit on the Black Tap menu. It's a burger, not a meatball parm, but it's inspired by my memories of summer Sundays when my mother and my aunt Donna would pack ten of us in two big cars to drive out to swim in the Long Island Sound. On the way home, we'd have dinner at different Italian restaurants, the kind with a pizza oven in the front and a dining room in the back. I always voted for a place in Yonkers called Pizza Beat and I always ordered their pizza burger. This tastes like those Sundays to me. *Food & Wine* magazine called this the ultimate hybrid burger!

BEST BEER: CONEY ISLAND MERMAID PILSNER, BROOKLYN, NEW YORK

Black Tap Tomato Sauce

- 1½ TABLESPOONS EXTRA-VIRGIN OLIVE OIL
- ¼ SMALL YELLOW ONION, FINELY CHOPPED
- 2 MEDIUM GARLIC CLOVES, THINLY SLICED
- 2 TABLESPOONS TOMATO PASTE
- 5 CUPS CRUSHED TOMATOES (FROM 1½ [28-OUNCE] CANS)
- 2 TEASPOONS KOSHER SALT
- ½ TEASPOON FRESHLY GROUND BLACK PEPPER

Burgers

- 2 POUNDS 80% LEAN GROUND BEEF
- 1 TABLESPOON KOSHER SALT
- ¼ TEASPOON FRESHLY GROUND BLACK PEPPER
- CANOLA OR VEGETABLE OIL FOR THE PAN
- FOUR ¼-INCH-THICK SLICES FRESH MOZZARELLA CHEESE
- FOUR 4-INCH POTATO BUNS
- 4 OUNCES PARMIGIANO-REGGIANO CHEESE, GRATED ON A MICROPLANE-STYLE RASP
- LETTUCE, TOMATO SLICES, PICKLE SPEARS, FOR SERVING

1 Heat the olive oil in a large saucepan over medium heat. Add the onion and garlic and cook, stirring often, until they are soft and translucent, 2 to 3 minutes. Stir in the tomato paste and cook, stirring often, until the color of the paste deepens, 3 to 4 minutes. Add the crushed tomatoes, increase the heat to medium-high, and cook, stirring continuously, until the sauce comes to a boil. Reduce the heat to low and cook, stirring often so nothing burns at the bottom, until the sauce has reduced by one-quarter, about 20 minutes. Season with the salt and pepper. (The sauce can be refrigerated in an airtight container or up to 1 week.)

2 Make the burgers: Place the ground beef in a large bowl and gently use your fingers to fluff the meat to loosen it (you don't want to overhandle the meat). Use a 4½- to 5-inch metal ring or your hands to make four ¾-inch-thick patties. Mix the salt and pepper together in a small bowl and use half of it to generously season the tops of the burger patties.

3 Heat a cast-iron flat-top griddle or large cast-iron skillet over medium-high heat for 2 minutes. Dip a folded paper towel in the oil and use it to grease the pan. With a spatula, carefully transfer the patties to the pan, seasoned-side down. Sprinkle the patties with the remaining salt and pepper mixture. Cook, without pressing down or moving the burgers, until the bottoms are browned, about 5 minutes. Flip the burgers and cook for 4½ to 5 minutes longer for medium-rare or 7 minutes more for medium. Spoon 2 tablespoons of the tomato sauce on to each burger and top with a slice of mozzarella. Add 1 teaspoon water to the pan, cover the pan immediately, and cook for about 10 seconds, until the cheese has melted, then transfer the burgers to a plate.

4 Pour out most of the fat from the pan and use a paper towel to wipe out the browned bits. Open the buns and place the bottom halves cut-side down in the hot pan until browned and toasted, 1 to 2 minutes. Turn the buns over to toast the other side, 30 seconds to 1 minute longer. Repeat with the bun tops.

5 Transfer each patty to a bottom bun half. Top with more tomato sauce and Parmigiano-Reggiano. Place the bun top on the burger and serve with lettuce, a tomato slice, and a pickle on the side.

THAT'S NICE

THE CHAMP

GREG NORMAN BURGER

SERVES 4

Black Tap won the People's Choice Award at the New York City Wine & Food Festival's Burger Bash with this special burger. We make it with Wagyu beef, a bit of blue cheese, baby arugula, and our Buttermilk-Dill Dressing. It's called the Greg Norman because he owns the Australian ranch that produces the terrific, funky Wagyu beef we use. If you've never cooked with Wagyu beef, give it a try; it's a flavorful, juicy meat with more monounsaturated fatty acids than regular beef, which means it's a little better for you, but that's just a bonus—it's really all about the smooth, rich flavor.

BEST BEER: BROOKLYN BREWERY BROOKLYN LAGER, BROOKLYN, NEW YORK

---

2 POUNDS GROUND KOBE-STYLE WAGYU BEEF

1½ TABLESPOONS PLUS ⅛ TEASPOON KOSHER SALT

½ TEASPOON PLUS A PINCH FRESHLY GROUND BLACK PEPPER

CANOLA OR VEGETABLE OIL FOR THE PAN

1 CUP CRUMBLED BLUE CHEESE

FOUR 4-INCH POTATO BUNS

1½ TEASPOONS EXTRA-VIRGIN OLIVE OIL

1½ TEASPOONS APPLE CIDER VINEGAR

1 CUP BABY ARUGULA

LETTUCE, TOMATO SLICES, PICKLE SPEARS, FOR SERVING

½ CUP BUTTERMILK-DILL DRESSING (page 66)

1 Place the beef in a large bowl and gently use your fingers to fluff the meat to loosen it (you don't want to overhandle the meat). Use a 4½- to 5-inch metal ring or your hands to make four ¾-inch-thick patties. Mix the 1½ tablespoons salt and ½ teaspoon pepper together in a small bowl and use half of it to generously season the tops of the burger patties.

2 Heat a cast-iron flat-top griddle or large cast-iron skillet over medium-high heat for 2 minutes. Dip a folded paper towel in oil and use it to grease the pan. Use a spatula to carefully transfer the patties to the pan and place them seasoned-side down. Sprinkle the patties with the remaining salt and pepper mixture. Cook, without pressing down or moving the burgers, until the bottoms are browned, about 5 minutes. Flip the burgers and cook for 4½ to 5 minutes longer for medium-rare or 7 minutes more for medium. Pat ¼ cup of the blue cheese onto each burger, add 1 teaspoon water to the pan, and cover the pan immediately. Cook for 10 seconds, until the cheese has melted, then transfer the burgers to a plate.

3 Pour off most of the fat from the pan and use a paper towel to wipe out the browned bits. Open the buns and place the bottom halves cut-side down in the hot pan until browned and toasted, 1 to 2 minutes. Turn the buns over to toast the other side, about 1 minute longer. Repeat with the bun tops.

4 Whisk the olive oil, vinegar, and the remaining salt and pepper together in a large bowl. Add the arugula and toss to coat. Place a burger on each bottom bun half and top with the arugula. Serve with lettuce, a tomato slice, and a pickle, with the Buttermilk-Dill Dressing on the side.

MEXICO CITY BURGER

SERVES 4

Don't confuse this with the Spicy Mexican (page 28), which is a ground pork burger with flavor notes you'd associate with a taco. This is a simple beef burger that gets different dimensions of flavor and heat from pepper Jack cheese, pickled jalapeños, and Chipotle Mayo. We amp it up with an onion ring for crunch and texture; onion rings also make a great side for this burger. (The Chipotle Mayo is my favorite dipping sauce when I eat the onion rings on their own, too.) If you have pickled red onions in the fridge, pile a few on as well! And enjoy this with an awesome Mexican soda like Jarrito.

BEST BEER: TECATE

Chipotle Mayo

½ CANNED CHIPOTLE CHILE IN ADOBO, PLUS ½ TEASPOON ADOBO SAUCE

¼ CUP MAYONNAISE

¼ TEASPOON GRATED LIME ZEST

SQUEEZE OF LIME JUICE

¾ TEASPOON WORCESTERSHIRE SAUCE

⅛ TEASPOON KOSHER SALT

Burgers

2 POUNDS 80% LEAN GROUND BEEF

1½ TABLESPOONS KOSHER SALT

½ TEASPOON FRESHLY GROUND BLACK PEPPER

CANOLA OR VEGETABLE OIL FOR THE PAN

8 SLICES SWISS CHEESE

FOUR 4-INCH POTATO BUNS

8 ONION RINGS (page 71)

PICKLED RED ONIONS (page 72), **OPTIONAL**

1 CUP PICKLED JALAPEÑOS

FRESH CILANTRO LEAVES

LETTUCE, TOMATO SLICES, PICKLE SPEARS, FOR SERVING

1 Place the chipotle chile and adobo sauce in a small bowl and use a fork to mash and stir them until it is a puree-like consistency. Add the mayonnaise, lime zest, lime juice, Worcestershire, and salt and stir to combine. Set aside.

2 Place the ground beef in a large bowl and gently use your fingers to fluff the meat to loosen it (you don't want to overhandle the meat). Use a 4½- to 5-inch metal ring or your hands to make four ¾-inch-thick patties. Mix the salt and pepper together in a small bowl and use half of it to generously season the tops of the burger patties.

3 Heat a cast-iron flat-top griddle or large cast-iron skillet over medium-high heat for 2 minutes. Dip a folded paper towel in oil and use it to grease the pan. With a spatula, carefully transfer the patties to the pan, seasoned-side down. Sprinkle the patties with the remaining salt and pepper mixture. Cook, without pressing down or moving the burgers, until the bottoms are browned, about 5 minutes. Flip the burgers and cook for 4½ to 5 minutes longer for medium-rare or 7 minutes more for medium. Tilt the pan to spoon out the excess fat if necessary after flipping. Place 2 slices of the cheese on each burger, add 1 teaspoon water to the pan, and cover the pan immediately. Cook for 10 seconds, until the cheese has melted, then transfer the burgers to a plate.

4 Pour off most of the fat from the pan and use a paper towel to wipe out the browned bits. Open the buns and place the bottom halves cut-side down in the hot pan until browned and toasted, 1 to 2 minutes. Turn the buns over to toast the other side, about 1 minute longer. Repeat with the bun tops.

5 Slide a patty onto each bun bottom and top with two Onion Rings, pickled jalapeños, pickled red onion, if using, and a few cilantro leaves. Divide the Chipotle Mayo among the top bun halves, place the bun tops on the burgers, and serve with lettuce, a tomato slice, and a pickle on the side.

SPICY!

SMOKY-SWEET

CAROLINA BURGER

SERVES 4 (WITH ABOUT 3¼ CUPS LEFTOVER BBQ SAUCE FOR YOUR NEXT COOKOUT)

If there is any food more American than a burger, it just might be barbecue, and our homage to the great North Carolina–style pulled pork sandwich combines both in one tangy, savory package. Our Carolina-style sauce gets a secret, savory kick from *gochujang* (a Korean chile paste well worth having in your kitchen). The combination of the seared ground beef and sweet, smoky pork gives you the best of both barbecue worlds. Serve it with coleslaw to complete the experience.

BEST BEER: THE CRISP, SIXPOINT BREWERY, BROOKLYN, NEW YORK

Carolina-Style BBQ Sauce

2 CUPS KETCHUP
¼ CUP CHILI POWDER
⅓ CUP LIGHTLY PACKED LIGHT BROWN SUGAR
½ CUP APPLE CIDER VINEGAR
2 TABLESPOONS SWEET PAPRIKA
2 TABLESPOONS WORCESTERSHIRE SAUCE
2 TABLESPOONS TABASCO SAUCE
2 TABLESPOONS GOCHUJANG (KOREAN CHILE PASTE)
1 TEASPOON FRESHLY GROUND BLACK PEPPER

Burgers

2 POUNDS 80% LEAN GROUND BEEF
1 TABLESPOON KOSHER SALT
¼ TEASPOON FRESHLY GROUND BLACK PEPPER
CANOLA OR VEGETABLE OIL FOR THE PAN
8 SLICES AMERICAN CHEESE
FOUR 4-INCH POTATO BUNS
½ POUND STORE-BOUGHT PULLED PORK
4 TABLESPOONS SPECIAL SAUCE (page 66)
½ POUND STORE-BOUGHT COLESLAW (ABOUT 1 CUP)
LETTUCE, TOMATO SLICES, PICKLE SPEARS, FOR SERVING

1 Stir the ketchup, chili powder, brown sugar, and ⅔ cup water together in a medium saucepan until well combined. Add the vinegar, paprika, Worcestershire, Tabasco, gochujang, and pepper, bring the sauce to a simmer over medium-high heat, then reduce the heat to medium-low and cook, stirring often, until it darkens and thickens slightly, 10 to 15 minutes (the vinegar taste may be very strong until the sauce is completely cooled). Let the sauce cool to room temperature.

2 Place the ground beef in a large bowl and gently use your fingers to fluff the meat to loosen it (you don't want to overhandle the meat). Use a 4½- to 5-inch metal ring or your hands to make four ¾-inch-thick patties. Mix the salt and pepper together in a small bowl and use half of it to generously season the tops of the burger patties.

3 Heat a cast-iron flat-top griddle or large cast-iron skillet over medium-high heat for 2 minutes. Dip a folded paper towel in oil and use it to grease the pan. Use a spatula to carefully transfer the patties to the pan, and place them seasoned-side down. Sprinkle the patties with the remaining salt and pepper mixture. Cook, without pressing down or moving the burgers, until the bottoms are browned, about 5 minutes. Flip the burgers and cook for 4½ to 5 minutes longer for medium-rare or 7 minutes more for medium. Place 2 slices of the cheese on each burger, add 1 teaspoon water to the pan, and cover the pan immediately. Cook for 10 seconds, until the cheese has melted, then transfer the burgers to a plate.

4 Pour off most of the fat from the pan and use a paper towel to wipe out the browned bits. Open the buns and place the bottom halves cut-side down in the hot pan until browned and toasted, 1 to 2 minutes. Turn the buns over to toast the other side, 30 seconds to 1 minute longer. Repeat with the bun tops.

5 Place the pulled pork in the pan and stir in ½ cup of the barbecue sauce. Stir over low heat until the pork is warmed through.

6 Transfer each patty to a bottom bun half and top with the pulled pork and some coleslaw. Spread 1 tablespoon of the Special Sauce on each top bun half and place the top buns on the burgers. Serve with more barbecue sauce on the side, along with lettuce, a tomato slice, and a pickle.

REUBEN BURGER

SERVES 4

Who doesn't love a Reuben, another New York diner classic? Like the Carolina, this is a pile-on. Serve it with onion rings and watch people go crazy, especially on St. Patty's Day.

BEST BEER: BLACK DUCK PORTER, GREENPORT HARBOR BREWING COMPANY, GREENPORT, NEW YORK, OR JUST GO WITH A TRADITIONAL PINT OF GUINNESS!

---

2 POUNDS 80% LEAN GROUND BEEF

1 TABLESPOON KOSHER SALT

¼ TEASPOON FRESHLY GROUND BLACK PEPPER

CANOLA OR VEGETABLE OIL FOR THE PAN

½ CUP DRAINED SAUERKRAUT

½ POUND THINLY SLICED CORNED BEEF

8 SLICES SWISS CHEESE

FOUR 4-INCH POTATO BUNS

1 CUP SPECIAL SAUCE (page 66)

LETTUCE, TOMATO SLICES, PICKLE SPEARS, FOR SERVING

1 Place the ground beef in a large bowl and gently use your fingers to fluff the meat to loosen it (you don't want to overhandle the meat). Use a 4½- to 5-inch metal ring or your hands to make four ¾-inch-thick patties. Mix the salt and pepper together in a small bowl and use half of it to generously season the tops of the burger patties.

2 Heat a cast-iron flat-top griddle or large cast-iron skillet over medium-high heat for 2 minutes. Dip a folded paper towel in oil and use it to grease the pan. Use a spatula to carefully transfer the patties to the pan and place them seasoned-side down. Sprinkle the patties with the remaining salt and pepper mixture. Cook, without pressing down or moving the burgers, until the bottoms are browned, about 5 minutes. Flip the burgers and cook for 4½ to 5 minutes longer for medium-rare or 7 minutes more for medium. Top each burger with one-quarter of the sauerkraut and cover with one-quarter of the corned beef and 2 slices of the cheese. Add 1 teaspoon water to the pan, cover the pan immediately, and cook for 10 seconds (or a few seconds longer, if your pan is large), until the cheese has melted, then transfer the burgers to a plate.

3 Pour off most of the fat from the pan and use a paper towel to wipe out the browned bits. Open the buns and place the bottom halves cut-side down in the hot pan until browned and toasted, 1 to 2 minutes. Turn the buns over to toast the other side, 30 seconds to 1 minute longer. Repeat with the bun tops.

4 Slide each patty onto a bun bottom. Divide the Special Sauce among the top bun halves and set them on top of the burgers. Serve with lettuce, a tomato slice, and a pickle on the side.

STACK THAT

KOBE-STYLE WAGYU

KOBE TRUFFLE BURGER

SERVES 4

This Kobe-style Wagyu beef burger is served with an unctuous black truffle mayonnaise and smoked gouda cheese. Don't skip the Japanese yuzu vinaigrette: its citrus cuts the richness while enhancing the flavor of this burger. When my niece Jolie decided to take a break from her vegetarian diet before an extended trip abroad, this was her pick—and what a way to start eating beef! Try it over greens tossed with some of the vinaigrette if you prefer to go bunless.

BEST BEER: SESSION IPA, BRONX BREWERY, BRONX, NEW YORK

Black Truffle Mayo

¼ CUP MAYONNAISE

¾ TEASPOON BLACK TRUFFLE OIL

PINCH OF FINELY GRATED LEMON ZEST

½ TEASPOON FRESH LEMON JUICE

1 TEASPOON FINELY CHOPPED BLACK TRUFFLE FROM A CAN (OPTIONAL)

Truffle Vinaigrette

1 TABLESPOON EXTRA-VIRGIN OLIVE OIL

1 TABLESPOON BLACK TRUFFLE OIL

2 TEASPOONS APPLE CIDER VINEGAR

2 TEASPOONS TAMARI

1½ TEASPOONS FRESH LEMON JUICE

1½ TEASPOONS BOTTLED YUZU JUICE (OR 1 TEASPOON LIME JUICE PLUS ¼ TEASPOON ORANGE JUICE AND ¼ TEASPOON LEMON JUICE)

Burgers

2 POUNDS GROUND KOBE-STYLE WAGYU BEEF

1½ TABLESPOONS KOSHER SALT

½ TEASPOON FRESHLY GROUND BLACK PEPPER

CANOLA OR VEGETABLE OIL FOR THE PAN

8 SLICES SMOKED GOUDA CHEESE

FOUR 4-INCH POTATO BUNS

1 CUP BABY ARUGULA

ONE 2-OUNCE WEDGE PARMIGIANO-REGGIANO CHEESE, GRATED ON A MICROPLANE-STYLE RASP

LETTUCE, TOMATO SLICES, PICKLE SPEARS, FOR SERVING

1 Whisk the mayonnaise, truffle oil, lemon zest, and lemon juice together in a small bowl until well combined. Stir in the chopped truffle, if using. Cover with plastic wrap and refrigerate for at least 2 hours and up to 1 week.

2 Whisk the olive oil, truffle oil, vinegar, tamari, lemon juice, and yuzu juice together in a medium bowl and set aside.

3 Place the ground beef in a large bowl and gently use your fingers to fluff the meat to loosen it (you don't want to overhandle the meat). Use a 4½- to 5-inch metal ring or your hands to make four ¾-inch-thick patties. Mix the salt and pepper together in a small bowl and use half of it to season the tops of the burger patties.

4 Heat a cast-iron flat-top griddle or large cast-iron skillet over medium-high heat for 2 minutes. Dip a folded paper towel in oil and use it to grease the pan. With a spatula, carefully transfer the patties to the pan, seasoned-side down. Sprinkle the patties with the remaining salt and pepper. Cook without pressing down or moving the burgers, until the bottoms are browned, about 5 minutes. Flip the burgers and cook until the other side is browned, about 5 minutes longer for medium-rare or 7 minutes longer for medium. Top each burger with 2 slices of the cheese, add 1 teaspoon water to the pan, and cover the pan immediately. Cook for 10 seconds (or a few seconds longer, if your pan is large), until the cheese has melted. Transfer the burgers to a plate.

5 Pour off most of the fat from the pan and use a paper towel to wipe out the browned bits. Open the buns and place the bottom halves cut-side down in the hot pan until browned and toasted, 1 to 2 minutes. Turn the buns over to toast the other side, 30 seconds to 1 minute longer. Repeat with the bun tops.

6 Add the arugula to the bowl with the Truffle Vinaigrette and toss to combine. Slide a patty onto each bun bottom. Divide the dressed greens among the burgers and top with the grated cheese. Smear the bun tops with the Truffle Mayo, set them on top of the burgers, and serve with lettuce, a tomato slice, and a pickle on the side.

THE NO BUN CLUB!

If you like burgers but prefer to eat healthy, consider losing the bun. These salads have all the great flavor and satisfying protein of our burgers but cut the carbs and increase the vegetables. It's easier to get a burger salad now than it was when we first started making them, but it's often just a burger plopped on top of a mess of greens. Black Tap salads are carefully composed, with vegetables, cheeses, and dressings that enhance the flavor of our craft burgers. These lighter preparations look fresh and provide a crisp, clean contrast to the unctuous burgers at their center. I'm continually surprised by how many kids order these salads, too. A few parents have told me that these combos have turned their skeptical kids into salad eaters!

BLACK TAP BURGER SALAD

SERVES 4

Back before Black Tap was even an idea, a friend and I double-dated at a Michelin-starred restaurant. Caesar salad and hamburgers were on the menu, but when our carb-conscious dates asked the server if they could skip the handmade brioche roll and have a burger served on top of a salad, this fancy restaurant refused. So the ladies simply took things into their own hands: they ordered two Caesars, two hamburgers, and created what they wanted at the table. I thought they were onto something. This low-carb, gluten-free indulgence was an immediate hit and featured in a lot of Black Tap's early press. If you are concerned about calories you can drop the bacon if you want, but do you? Really?

2 POUNDS 80% LEAN GROUND BEEF

1 TABLESPOON PLUS ⅛ TEASPOON KOSHER SALT

¼ TEASPOON PLUS A PINCH FRESHLY GROUND BLACK PEPPER

CANOLA OR VEGETABLE OIL FOR THE PAN

8 SLICES AMERICAN CHEESE

8 SLICES APPLEWOOD-SMOKED BACON, COOKED UNTIL CRISP

2 TABLESPOONS EXTRA-VIRGIN OLIVE OIL

2 TABLESPOONS APPLE CIDER VINEGAR

6 CUPS GREEN-LEAF LETTUCE, WASHED AND COARSELY TORN

8 SCALLIONS, GREEN AND WHITE PARTS, FINELY CHOPPED

⅔ CUP PICKLED RED ONIONS (page 72)

1 CUP HALVED GRAPE TOMATOES

½ CUP CHOPPED CUCUMBER

4 PICKLE SPEARS, OPTIONAL

1 CUP SPECIAL SAUCE (page 66)

1 Place the ground beef in a large bowl and gently use your fingers to fluff the meat to loosen it (you don't want to overhandle the meat). Use a 4½- to 5-inch metal ring or your hands to make four ¾-inch-thick patties. Mix 1 tablespoon of the salt and ¼ teaspoon of the pepper together in a small bowl and use half of it to season the tops of the burger patties.

2 Heat a cast-iron flat-top griddle or large cast-iron skillet over medium-high heat for 2 minutes. Dip a folded paper towel in oil and use it to grease the pan. Use a spatula to carefully transfer the patties to the pan seasoned-side down. Sprinkle the patties with the remaining salt and pepper mixture. Cook, without pressing down or moving the burgers, until the bottoms are browned, about 5 minutes. Flip the burgers and cook for 4½ to 5 minutes longer for medium-rare or 7 minutes for medium. Place 2 slices of the cheese on each burger, add 1 teaspoon water to the pan, and cover the pan immediately. Cook for 10 seconds, until the cheese has melted, then transfer the burgers to a plate.

3 Whisk the olive oil, vinegar, and remaining ⅛ teaspoon salt and pinch of pepper together in a large bowl. Add the lettuce and toss to coat with the dressing, then divide the dressed greens among four salad bowls. Sprinkle each serving with the scallions, pickled onions, grape tomatoes, and cucumber. Set a pickle spear on the side of each if you like. Top each salad with a burger and 2 bacon strips and serve with a small dish of Special Sauce on the side.

TURKEY BURGER SALAD

SERVES 4

I get a kick out of all the local ladies who come into our noisy burger joint with their yoga mats after class to order this salad, our most popular. It's an approachable, healthy mix of tastes and textures that includes two superfoods: kale and avocado. The mixture of lettuces is important for balance in this salad. The Granny Smith apples should be crisp and tart, for texture and acidity. Don't skip the dried cranberries; they add just the right amount of sweetness and chew. Crumbled blue cheese adds a bit of extra protein and substance.

1 POUND GROUND WHITE-MEAT TURKEY

1 POUND GROUND DARK-MEAT TURKEY

1 TABLESPOON PLUS ⅛ TEASPOON KOSHER SALT

¼ TEASPOON PLUS A PINCH FRESHLY GROUND BLACK PEPPER

CANOLA OR VEGETABLE OIL FOR THE PAN

3 CUPS TORN GREEN-LEAF LETTUCE

3 CUPS FINELY CHOPPED KALE OR BABY KALE

2 TABLESPOONS EXTRA-VIRGIN OLIVE OIL

2 TABLESPOONS APPLE CIDER VINEGAR

½ CUP DRIED CRANBERRIES

2 GRANNY SMITH APPLES, HALVED, CORED, AND FINELY CHOPPED

2 CUPS CRUMBLED BLUE CHEESE

2 HASS AVOCADOS, HALVED, PITTED, PEELED, AND SLICED OR CHOPPED

1 CUP BUTTERMILK-DILL DRESSING (page 66)

1 Place all the ground turkey in a large bowl and gently use your fingers to fluff the mixture to loosen the meat and combine the light and dark meat together as best as you can (you don't want to overhandle the meat). Use a 4½- to 5-inch metal ring or your hands to make four ¾-inch-thick patties. Mix 1 tablespoon of the salt and ¼ teaspoon of the pepper together in a small bowl and use half of it to season the tops of the burger patties.

2 Heat a cast-iron flat-top griddle or large cast-iron skillet over medium-high heat for 2 minutes. Dip a folded paper towel in oil and use it to grease the pan. Use a spatula to carefully transfer the patties to the pan and place them seasoned-side down. Season the patties with the remaining salt and pepper mixture. Cook, without pressing down on the burgers, until both sides are browned and the internal temperature of a patty registers 165°F on an instant-read thermometer, 12 to 14 minutes total, turning the burgers midway through the cooking time. Transfer the burgers to a plate.

3 Put the lettuce and kale in a large bowl. Whisk the olive oil, vinegar, and remaining ⅛ teaspoon salt and pinch of pepper together in a small bowl. Drizzle the vinaigrette over the greens and toss to coat, then divide the dressed greens among four salad bowls. Sprinkle with the dried cranberries, apples, half the cheese, and the avocado. Place a burger on each salad and top with more cheese. Serve with the Buttermilk-Dill Dressing on the side.

HEY, LADIES

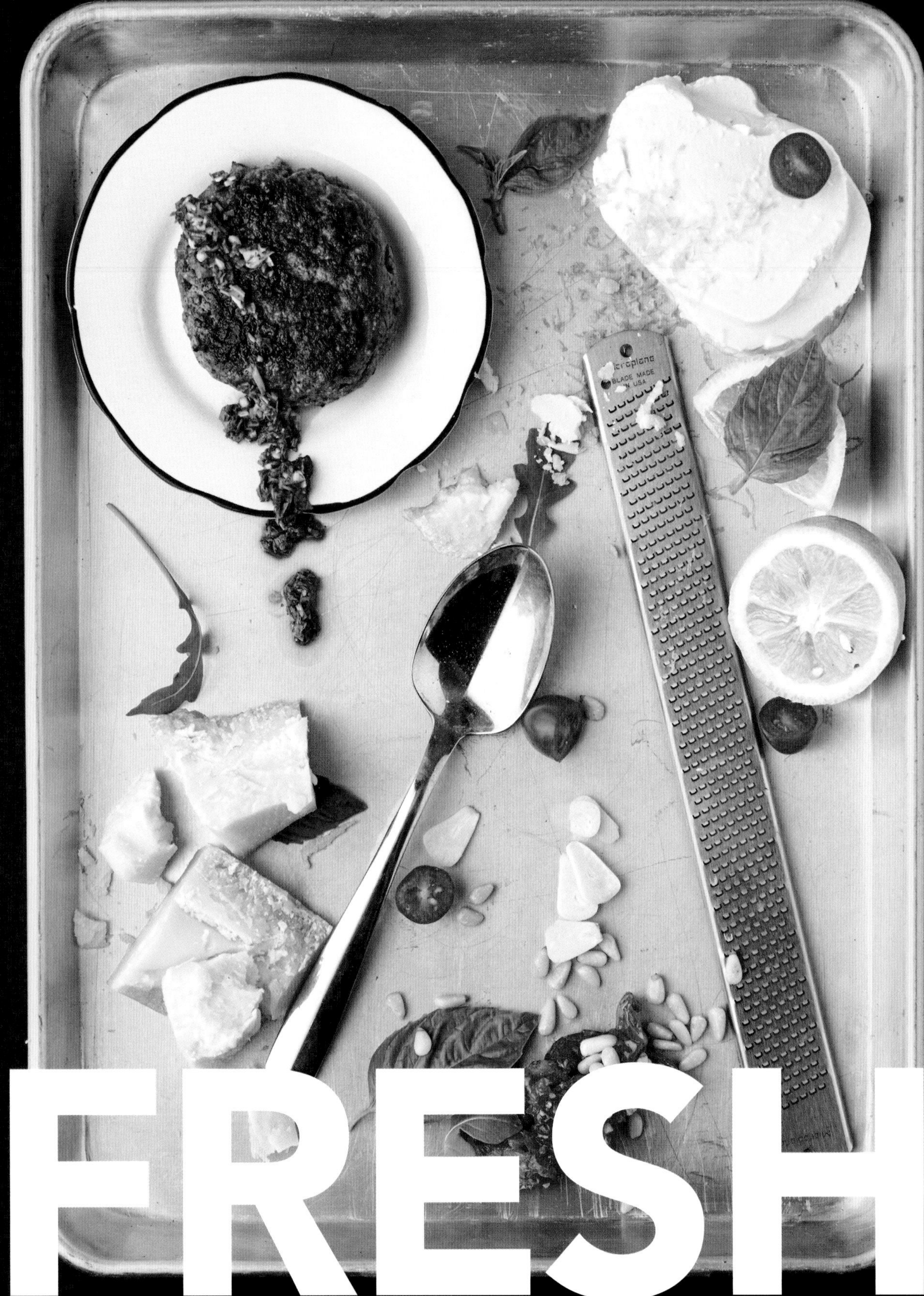

FRESH

BISON BURGER SALAD

SERVES 4

Some people love bison for the flavor, which is similar to beef, and others choose bison because it makes a burger that is lower in fat, calories, and cholesterol. You'll want to make this Italian-inspired salad both because it's an even lighter, healthier way to serve this sophisticated burger—and because it just tastes great.

Chimichurri Sauce

¼ CUP FINELY CHOPPED FLAT-LEAF PARSLEY LEAVES
¼ CUP FINELY CHOPPED FRESH BASIL
½ SMALL RED ONION, FINELY CHOPPED
3 GARLIC CLOVES, FINELY CHOPPED
½ CUP EXTRA-VIRGIN OLIVE OIL
¼ CUP APPLE CIDER VINEGAR
¼ TEASPOON KOSHER SALT
PINCH OF FRESHLY GROUND BLACK PEPPER

Burger Salad

¼ CUP PINE NUTS
1½ POUNDS GROUND BISON
1 TABLESPOON PLUS ⅛ TEASPOON KOSHER SALT
¼ TEASPOON PLUS A PINCH FRESHLY GROUND BLACK PEPPER
CANOLA OR VEGETABLE OIL FOR THE PAN
4 ROASTED TOMATOES, STORE-BOUGHT OR HOMEMADE (page 36)
2 TABLESPOONS EXTRA-VIRGIN OLIVE OIL
2 TABLESPOONS APPLE CIDER VINEGAR
6 CUPS BABY ARUGULA
1 CUP HALVED GRAPE TOMATOES
½ POUND FRESH MOZZARELLA, CUT INTO BITE-SIZE PIECES
ONE 2-OUNCE CHUNK PARMIGIANO-REGGIANO CHEESE, GRATED ON A MICROPLANE-STYLE RASP

1 Whisk together the parsley, cilantro, onion, garlic, olive oil, vinegar, salt, and pepper in a small bowl. Set 1 cup aside and transfer the rest to an airtight container and refrigerate for up to 5 days.

2 Place the pine nuts in a small skillet and toast over medium heat, shaking the pan often, until they are golden brown, 4 to 5 minutes. Transfer to a small plate to cool.

3 Place the bison in a large bowl and gently use your fingers to fluff the meat to loosen it (you don't want to overhandle the meat). Use a 4- to 4½-inch metal ring or your hands to make four ½- to ¾-inch-thick patties. Mix 1 tablespoon of the salt and ¼ teaspoon of the pepper together in a small bowl and use half of it to season the tops of the burger patties.

4 Heat a cast-iron flat-top griddle or large cast-iron skillet over medium-high heat for 2 minutes. Dip a folded paper towel in oil and use it to grease the pan. Use a spatula to carefully transfer the patties to the pan and place them seasoned-side down. Season the patties with the remaining salt and pepper mixture and cook until browned, about 5 minutes. Flip the burgers and cook for 4 to 5 minutes for medium-rare and 5 to 6 minutes for medium. Transfer the burgers to a plate.

5 Add the roasted tomatoes to the pan and cook until warmed through, 1 to 2 minutes, turning them once.

6 Whisk the olive oil, vinegar, remaining ⅛ teaspoon salt and pinch of pepper together in a large bowl. Add the arugula and toss to coat. Divide the dressed greens among four salad bowls and sprinkle each with the grape tomatoes, mozzarella, and toasted pine nuts. Top each with a burger and a roasted tomato. Drizzle each salad with some Chimichurri Sauce and finish with the Parmigiano-Reggiano.

GREEK BURGER SALAD WITH SWEET LEMON DRESSING

SERVES 4

Mediterranean flavors go global in this salad, which features a lamb burger topped with a special lemon dressing. The dressing looks and tastes creamy but has no dairy at all. It adds an unexpected dimension of sweetness that complements the savory lamb and salty feta. Our customers love it!

Sweet Lemon Dressing

1½ LEMONS

½ CUP COARSE RAW SUGAR SUCH AS SUGAR IN THE RAW

2 TABLESPOONS CANOLA OR VEGETABLE OIL

Burger Salad

1½ TEASPOONS CURRY POWDER

1½ TEASPOONS CHINESE FIVE-SPICE POWDER

1½ POUNDS GROUND LAMB

1 TABLESPOON PLUS ¼ TEASPOON KOSHER SALT

¼ TEASPOON PLUS A PINCH FRESHLY GROUND BLACK PEPPER

CANOLA OR VEGETABLE OIL FOR THE PAN

2 TABLESPOONS OLIVE OIL

2 TABLESPOONS RED WINE VINEGAR

6 CUPS TORN GREEN-LEAF LETTUCE

1 CUP HALVED GRAPE TOMATOES

1 CUP FINELY CHOPPED CUCUMBER

½ CUP PICKLED RED ONIONS (page 72)

1 CUP PITTED KALAMATA OLIVES (ABOUT 4 OUNCES)

1 CUP CRUMBLED FETA CHEESE (ABOUT 4 OUNCES)

1 Slice the whole lemon into quarters. Add ½ cup of water and the sugar to a small saucepan and bring to a boil over high heat. Add the lemon quarters to the sugar syrup, reduce the heat to medium-low, cover, and gently cook the lemons, stirring often and reducing the heat if necessary, until the skins are soft, 10 to 15 minutes. Turn off the heat and let the lemons cool in the syrup. The poached lemons can be transferred to an airtight container and refrigerated for up to 1 week.

2 Remove any seeds from the poached lemons and add the lemon quarters along with 2 tablespoons of the lemon poaching liquid to a blender. Juice the remaining lemon half and add 2 tablespoons of the juice to the blender. Blend on high speed until combined and smooth. Reduce the speed to low and add the oil in a slow, steady stream until the dressing is emulsified and thick. The dressing can be refrigerated in an airtight container for up to 1 week.

3 Mix the curry and five-spice powders in a small bowl and set aside. Place the ground lamb in a large bowl and gently use your fingers to fluff the lamb to loosen it (you don't want to overhandle the meat). Use a 4- to 4½-inch metal ring or your hands to make four ¾-inch-thick patties. Mix 1 tablespoon of the salt and ¼ teaspoon of the pepper together in a small bowl and use half of it to generously season the tops of the burger patties, then sprinkle the patties with half the curry mixture.

4 Heat a cast-iron flat-top griddle or large cast-iron skillet over medium-high heat for 2 minutes. Dip a folded paper towel in oil and use it to grease the pan. With a spatula, carefully transfer the patties to the pan, seasoned-side down. Sprinkle the patties with the remaining salt and pepper mixture and remaining curry mixture. Cook, without pressing down or moving the burgers, until the bottoms are browned, 4 to 5 minutes. Flip the patties and cook for 4 to 5 minutes longer for medium-rare or 7 minutes more for medium. Transfer the burgers to a plate.

5 In a large bowl, whisk together the olive oil, vinegar, remaining ¼ teaspoon salt and pinch of pepper. Add the lettuce and toss to coat, then divide among four bowls. Top each salad with one-quarter of the tomatoes, cucumber, pickled onions, and olives. Divide half the feta cheese among the bowls. Place a lamb patty on each salad and finish with the remaining feta cheese. Serve with the Sweet Lemon Dressing on the side.

LEMONY

GREEN

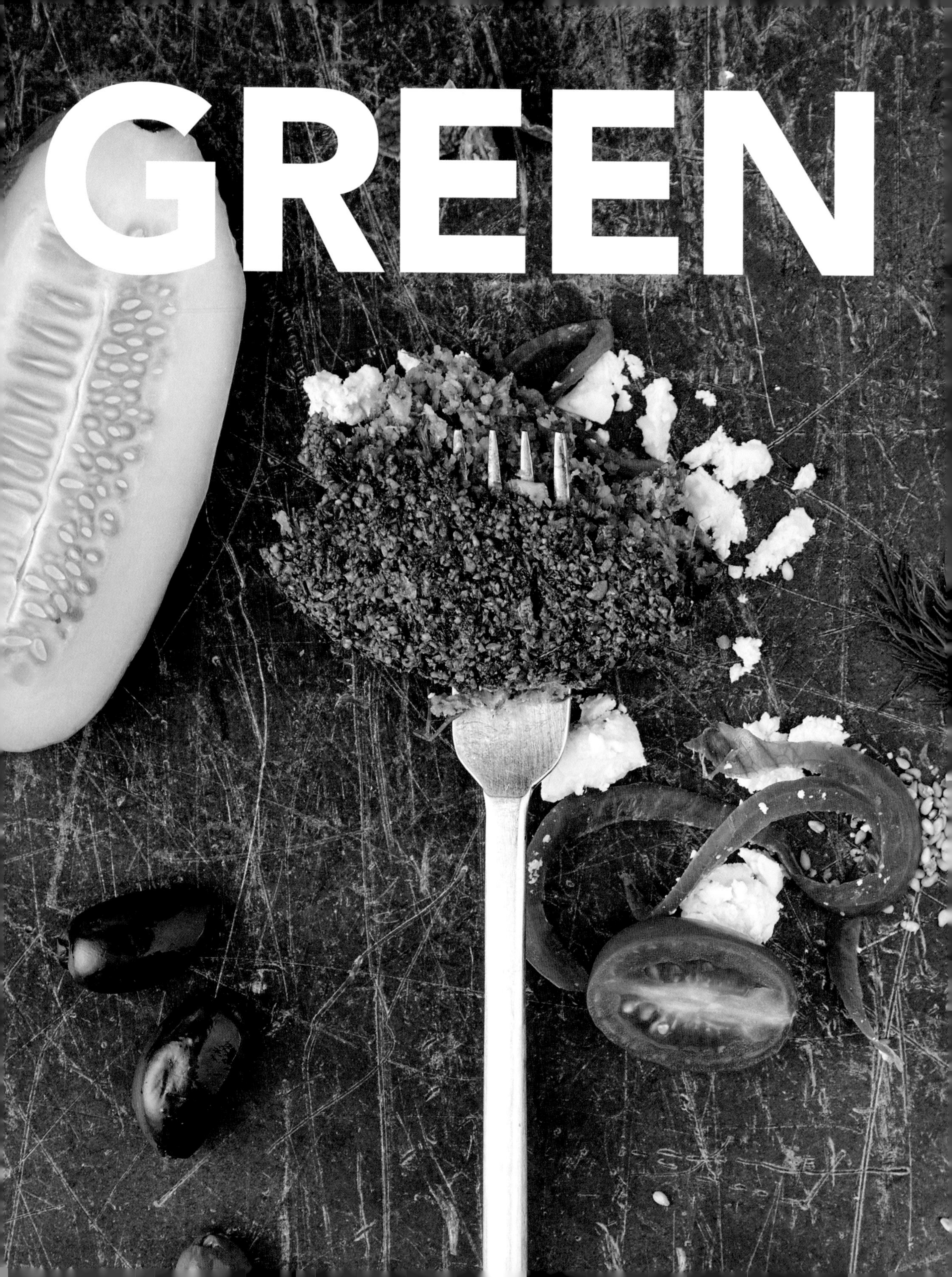

FALAFEL BURGER SALAD

SERVES 4

Michael Schwartz, the chef-owner of Miami's famed Michael's Genuine Food & Drink, and I were two East Coast guys working in Miami and missing our childhood street foods when we came up with this falafel. I've had it on the menu in some form at every place I've worked since. It's a zingier, more herbaceous, lighter style of falafel than what you might expect, and in this salad, it's served over classic accompaniments like tomato, cucumber, pickled onions, roasted eggplant, scallions, and feta cheese. We serve it with a tahini dressing. If you omit the cheese, you have a fully vegan, gluten-free option for dinner.

Tahini Sauce

2 TABLESPOONS TAHINI (SESAME PASTE)
¼ CUP TAMARI
¼ CUP APPLE CIDER VINEGAR
¾ TEASPOON FRESH LEMON JUICE
¼ CUP CANOLA OR VEGETABLE OIL
¼ CUP CHILI OIL (page 67)

Burger Salad

2 TABLESPOONS APPLE CIDER VINEGAR
2 TABLESPOONS EXTRA-VIRGIN OLIVE OIL
⅛ TEASPOON KOSHER SALT
PINCH OF FRESHLY GROUND BLACK PEPPER
6 CUPS GREEN-LEAF LETTUCE, COARSELY TORN
1 CUP HALVED GRAPE TOMATOES
1 CUP FINELY CHOPPED CUCUMBERS
1 CUP DRAINED PICKLED RED ONIONS (page 72)
½ CUP PITTED KALAMATA OLIVES
1 CUP CRUMBLED FETA CHEESE
½ CUP HUMMUS (page 67)
4 FRIED FALAFEL BURGERS (page 32)

1 To a blender jar, add the ingredients in this order: tahini, tamari, vinegar, and lemon juice. Blend on medium speed, then with the motor running, slowly drizzle in the canola oil and chili oil. Blend until completely smooth. The dressing can be used immediately or refrigerated in an airtight container for up to 5 days.

2 Whisk the vinegar, olive oil, salt, and pepper together in a large bowl, add the lettuce, and toss to combine. Divide the salad among four bowls.

3 Arrange the tomatoes, cucumbers, half the pickled onions, the olives, and half the feta cheese on top. Dollop the hummus onto each salad. Set one cooked falafel patty on top of the hummus in each bowl, top with the remaining pickled onions, then sprinkle each falafel patty with some of the remaining feta cheese. Serve with the Tahini Sauce on the side.

SAUCES & SIDES

Sauces are part of the Black Tap DNA. Sauces create the unique flavor profiles of our burgers, and they round out and elevate the flavors of our salads and sides. And who doesn't enjoy french fries and onion rings with an awesome dipping sauce?

Every burger at Black Tap comes with a sauce, and if you make and use the sauces properly, you'll never need ketchup. We make most of our sauces by hand daily, and it's worth your time to make them, too. They aren't complicated, and when you compare most sauces you make from scratch to premade, packaged products, you'll taste a difference.

That said, the difference is in the details, but we do use some commercial products in our sauces, either because I think someone else is making something so great that I don't want to mess with it, or because we can't make a consistently fantastic alternative at the volume we would need in the restaurant. If you want to make your own ketchup, knock yourself out, but we use Heinz ketchup, along with Sweet Baby Ray's BBQ sauce, and Kraft mayonnaise. We call them mother sauces, and the iconic tastes of those products are part of the old-school luncheonette experience that inspires me.

We also offer a short list of classic and not-so-classic accompaniments for our burgers, including fries and onion rings that are anything but run of the mill. Balance out these golden brown and delicious beauties with some gorgeous green broccoli or Brussels sprouts, top your burger with pickled onions or a dollop of Mexican Avocado, and all is right with the world.

SPECIAL SAUCE

MAKES 1⅓ CUPS

½ CUP MAYONNAISE

MOUNDED ⅓ CUP KETCHUP

2 TABLESPOONS WORCESTERSHIRE SAUCE

1½ TABLESPOONS MASHED CANNED CHIPOTLE CHILE IN ADOBO SAUCE (ABOUT ½ CHILE), PLUS 1 TABLESPOON ADOBO SAUCE

¼ TEASPOON GOCHUJANG (KOREAN CHILE PASTE)

1½ TEASPOONS FINELY CHOPPED HALF-SOUR PICKLE

¾ TEASPOON PICKLE BRINE (FROM THE JAR)

Place the mayonnaise, ketchup, Worcestershire sauce, chipotle, chile paste, pickle, and pickle brine in a medium bowl and whisk to combine. Cover the bowl with plastic wrap and refrigerate for at least 2 hours to let the flavors come together. The sauce keeps in the refrigerator for up to 6 days.

PICO DE GALLO

MAKES 3 CUPS

2 MEDIUM TOMATOES, CORED AND FINELY CHOPPED

¼ MEDIUM SPANISH ONION, FINELY CHOPPED

½ CUP FINELY CHOPPED JALAPEÑOS, SEEDED FOR LESS HEAT, IF DESIRED

¼ CUP FINELY CHOPPED FRESH CILANTRO LEAVES, OR MORE TO TASTE

1½ TEASPOONS KOSHER SALT

1½ TEASPOONS FRESHLY GROUND BLACK PEPPER

1½ TABLESPOONS DISTILLED WHITE VINEGAR OR APPLE CIDER VINEGAR

3 TABLESPOONS EXTRA-VIRGIN OLIVE OIL

JUICE OF 1 LIME, OR MORE TO TASTE

Place the tomatoes, onion, jalapeños, cilantro, salt, and pepper in a medium bowl and stir to combine. Add the vinegar, olive oil, and lime juice and mix. Taste and add more cilantro or lime juice to taste if you want a richer flavor and more body. Serve immediately or refrigerate in an airtight container for up to 3 days (but note that it is best served within 24 hours of making).

BUTTERMILK-DILL DRESSING

MAKES 1½ CUPS

1 CUP MAYONNAISE

½ CUP BUTTERMILK

1 TABLESPOON FINELY CHOPPED FRESH DILL

¼ TEASPOON GARLIC POWDER

¼ TEASPOON ONION POWDER

½ TEASPOON KOSHER SALT (OPTIONAL)

Whisk the mayonnaise, buttermilk, dill, garlic powder, and onion powder together in a medium bowl. Taste and add the salt, if needed. Transfer to an airtight container and refrigerate for at least 2 hours before using. The dressing can be refrigerated for up to 1 week.

HUMMUS

MAKES 2½ CUPS

3 CUPS COOKED CHICKPEAS (CANNED OR COOKED FROM DRIED CHICKPEAS)

1 CUP TAHINI SAUCE (page 63)

2 TABLESPOONS FRESH LEMON JUICE

½ CUP EXTRA-VIRGIN OLIVE OIL, PLUS MORE AS NEEDED

¼ TEASPOON KOSHER SALT

PINCH OF FRESHLY GROUND BLACK PEPPER

Add the chickpeas, Tahini Sauce, lemon juice, olive oil, salt, and pepper to the bowl of a food processor and process until smooth. Taste and add more olive oil for a richer flavor, if you like. Serve at room temperature or chilled. Store in an airtight container in the refrigerator for up to 5 days.

CHILI OIL

MAKES ¾ CUP

½ CUP CANOLA OR VEGETABLE OIL

¼ CUP EXTRA-VIRGIN OLIVE OIL

1 TABLESPOON CHILI POWDER

1 TABLESPOON SWEET SMOKED PAPRIKA (PIMENTÓN)

Combine the canola oil and olive oil in a small saucepan and place over medium heat until warm, about 5 minutes. Add the chili powder and paprika, turn off the heat immediately, and set aside to cool to room temperature. Pour into an airtight container and store in a cool, dark, and dry spot for up to 1 week.

KOREAN BBQ SAUCE

MAKES 1½ CUPS

1 CUP CAROLINA-STYLE BBQ SAUCE (page 47) **OR YOUR FAVORITE BARBECUE SAUCE**

¼ CUP STORE-BOUGHT BOTTLED KIMCHI BASE OR LIQUID FROM PREPARED KIMCHI

2 TABLESPOONS SRIRACHA

2 TABLESPOONS TOASTED SESAME OIL

2 TABLESPOONS FRESH LIME JUICE (FROM 1 OR 2 LIMES)

Whisk together the barbecue sauce, kimchi base, Sriracha, sesame oil, and lime juice in a large bowl. The barbecue sauce can be refrigerated for up to 1 week in an airtight container.

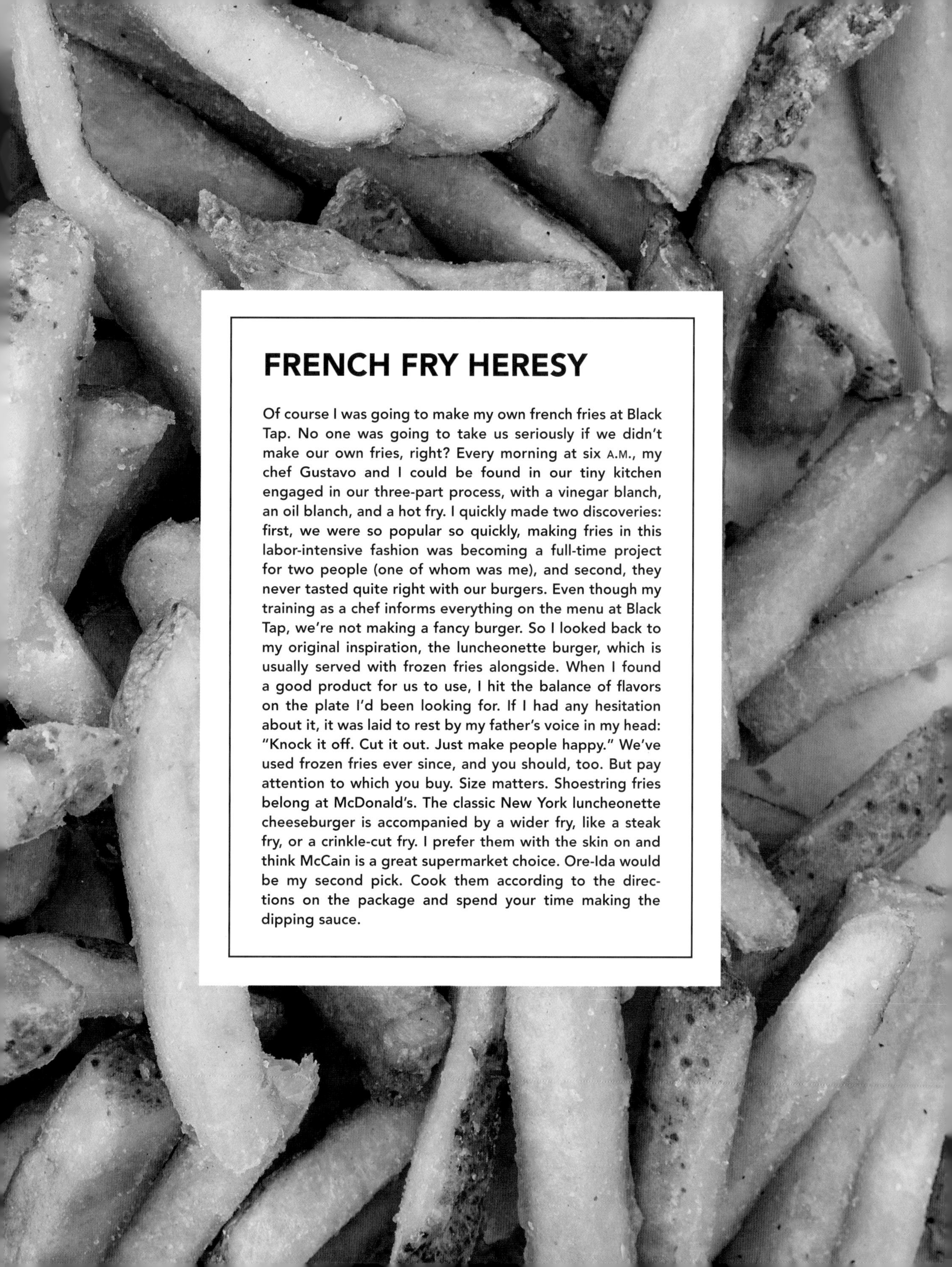

FRENCH FRY HERESY

Of course I was going to make my own french fries at Black Tap. No one was going to take us seriously if we didn't make our own fries, right? Every morning at six A.M., my chef Gustavo and I could be found in our tiny kitchen engaged in our three-part process, with a vinegar blanch, an oil blanch, and a hot fry. I quickly made two discoveries: first, we were so popular so quickly, making fries in this labor-intensive fashion was becoming a full-time project for two people (one of whom was me), and second, they never tasted quite right with our burgers. Even though my training as a chef informs everything on the menu at Black Tap, we're not making a fancy burger. So I looked back to my original inspiration, the luncheonette burger, which is usually served with frozen fries alongside. When I found a good product for us to use, I hit the balance of flavors on the plate I'd been looking for. If I had any hesitation about it, it was laid to rest by my father's voice in my head: "Knock it off. Cut it out. Just make people happy." We've used frozen fries ever since, and you should, too. But pay attention to which you buy. Size matters. Shoestring fries belong at McDonald's. The classic New York luncheonette cheeseburger is accompanied by a wider fry, like a steak fry, or a crinkle-cut fry. I prefer them with the skin on and think McCain is a great supermarket choice. Ore-Ida would be my second pick. Cook them according to the directions on the package and spend your time making the dipping sauce.

PUT A RING ON IT

ONION RINGS

SERVES 4

At Black Tap, we love to put a ring on it. They add texture and flavor to some of our burgers, but they are special on their own. Unlike french fries, there are no acceptable options for frozen onion rings, which are uniformly overbreaded, bland, and mealy. Fortunately, onion rings are simple to make at home and well worth it. You do need a thermometer if you don't have a countertop fryer, like a FryDaddy, to make sure you keep a steady temperature and have the oil exactly where you need it to be before cooking each batch. Always and only use Spanish onion, soaked in buttermilk for a few hours, and dredged in a mix of all-purpose flour and Wondra flour, before frying to a light, shattering, nongreasy crisp. Chipotle Mayo (page 44) is my favorite accompaniment.

2½ CUPS BUTTERMILK

2½ TEASPOONS KOSHER SALT

1 LARGE SPANISH ONION (ABOUT 1¼ POUNDS), SLICED INTO ½-INCH-THICK RINGS

2 CUPS WONDRA FLOUR

⅔ CUP ALL-PURPOSE FLOUR

2 TEASPOONS FRESHLY GROUND BLACK PEPPER

1 Whisk the buttermilk and ½ teaspoon of the salt together in a baking dish. Add the onions and spread them out so they are more or less in a single layer and covered with the buttermilk (there may be a few that poke up through the buttermilk). Set aside at room temperature for 30 minutes, turning the onions occasionally so any that were not totally submerged get a chance to be covered by buttermilk.

2 Heat the oil in a large saucepan set over high heat until it reads 350°F on an instant-read thermometer. Reduce the heat to medium-high to maintain a 350°F temperature. Set a wire rack on a rimmed baking sheet and set aside.

3 Whisk the Wondra flour, all-purpose flour, remaining 2 teaspoons salt, and the pepper together in a medium bowl. Lift a few of the onions out of the buttermilk, letting the excess drain off. Place them in the flour mixture and dredge them to coat all sides. Return them to the buttermilk for a quick dunk, lift them out, and dredge through the flour again. Shake off the excess, then carefully drop them into the hot oil (don't add too many at once or they will stick together). Fry the onion rings until they are golden brown and the bubbles surrounding the onions subside, about 2 minutes. Use a slotted spoon or frying spider to transfer them to the wire rack to cool. Repeat with the remaining onions, adjusting the heat up or down to maintain 350°F. Serve the onion rings hot.

PICKLED RED ONIONS

MAKES 1½ QUARTS

These add just the right sharp bite to so many dishes, especially those that are on the rich side. Pile them onto a burger, sprinkle them on a fish taco, or use them to brighten an earthy salad, like our Roasted Beets with blue cheese. They keep for a long time in the fridge, so make them in quantity; you'll find a million ways to use them.

2½ POUNDS RED ONIONS (ABOUT 6 MEDIUM ONIONS)
1 LARGE RED BEET, QUARTERED
2 CUPS APPLE CIDER VINEGAR
¼ CUP SUGAR
¼ CUP KOSHER SALT
3 STAR ANISE
1 CINNAMON STICK

1 Slice the onions very thinly crosswise into rings using a mandoline or sharp chef's knife. Place the onions in a large bowl with the beets.

2 Bring 6 cups water to a boil in a medium pot. Add the vinegar, sugar, salt, star anise, and cinnamon stick, return the liquid to a simmer, and stir until the sugar and salt have dissolved. Turn off the heat and pour the hot pickling liquid over the onions and beets. Stir the mixture and set aside to cool to room temperature, 2 to 3 hours.

3 Cover the bowl with plastic wrap and refrigerate for at least 1 hour or preferably overnight. Use tongs to transfer the onions to airtight containers or glass pickling jars. (You can discard the beets if your onions are tinted to your liking or store them along with the onions to deepen the color; discard them once the onions are used up.) Top off the jars with some of the pickling liquid. The onions will keep in the refrigerator for up to 1 month.

TERIYAKI BROCCOLI

SERVES 4

My dad and I loved eating Chinese food on our culinary outings, especially chicken and broccoli in spicy garlic sauce, which inspired this side. This dish starts with the ginger, garlic, and scallion trinity that make a kind of Asian mirepoix and are the foundation of what will taste like the greatest Chinese takeout you've ever ordered. We sauté the broccoli with these aromatics in sesame oil, and finish it with a teriyaki glaze, a bit of fresh lemon juice, and a touch of butter. Everyone eats their vegetables these days, and this a nice, healthier side for your burgers and fries.

3 TABLESPOONS CANOLA OR VEGETABLE OIL

1½ POUNDS BITE-SIZE BROCCOLI FLORETS

4 GARLIC CLOVES, THINLY SLICED

2 TABLESPOONS FINELY CHOPPED FRESH GINGER

½ CUP STORE-BOUGHT TERIYAKI SAUCE

2 TABLESPOONS FRESH LEMON JUICE

2 SCALLIONS, WHITE AND LIGHT GREEN PARTS, THINLY SLICED ON AN ANGLE

1 Heat the oil in a large, deep skillet over medium-high heat for 2 minutes. Add the broccoli and cook, stirring occasionally, until it is bright green and beginning to turn golden brown in places, 3 to 5 minutes.

2 Stir in the garlic and ginger and cook, stirring often, until the broccoli is tender, 2 to 3 minutes.

3 Stir in the teriyaki sauce and lemon juice and bring to a simmer. Turn off the heat and transfer the broccoli to a platter. Serve sprinkled with the scallions.

ROASTED BEETS

SERVES 4

Call this a salad, a side, or even a condiment, but try it once and you'll call it one of your favorites.

4 LARGE BEETS

3 TABLESPOONS EXTRA-VIRGIN OLIVE OIL, PLUS MORE FOR ROASTING THE BEETS

KOSHER SALT AND FRESHLY GROUND BLACK PEPPER TO TASTE

¼ CUP PICKLED RED ONIONS (page 72)

1 TABLESPOON MINCED SCALLION, WHITE AND GREEN PARTS

1 TABLESPOON APPLE CIDER VINEGAR

1 CUP BUTTERMILK-DILL DRESSING (page 66)

1 OUNCE CRUMBLED BLUE CHEESE

1 Preheat the oven to 400°F.

2 Clean the beets by scrubbing thoroughly under running water. Dry completely. Place the beets in a foil-lined baking pan. Lightly coat the beets with olive oil and season with salt and pepper. Fill the pan with ½ inch of water, then cover the baking pan tightly with foil. Roast the beets for 50 to 60 minutes, or until you can insert a fork without resistance.

3 While still warm, peel the beets, using a clean dish towel to protect your hands from staining. Cut the beets into irregular 1½-inch pieces and place in a large mixing bowl. Add the pickled red onions and scallions. Lightly dress with the vinegar, the 3 tablespoons of olive oil, and salt and pepper to taste.

4 Pour the Buttermilk-Dill Dressing onto a rimmed serving platter and top with the beets. Sprinkle with the blue cheese and serve.

SO
FRESH
SO
CLEAN

CRISPY BRUSSELS SPROUTS

SERVES 4

The WingBar in the Carroll Gardens section of Brooklyn makes a great burger, but I go there for the sprouts. The addictive smell of WingBar sprouts tossed in a sweet-and-sour vinegar mixture makes me float toward them like Pepé Le Pew every time I'm in the neighborhood. At Black Tap, we flash-fry our sprouts, toss them with salt and pepper, and serve them with our homemade Tahini Sauce.

8 CUPS CANOLA OR VEGETABLE OIL, FOR FRYING

1¼ POUNDS BRUSSELS SPROUTS, HALVED (MAKE SURE THEY ARE COMPLETELY DRY)

¼ TEASPOON KOSHER SALT

⅛ TEASPOON FRESHLY GROUND BLACK PEPPER

TAHINI SAUCE (page 63), **FOR SERVING**

Heat the oil in a large deep pot over medium-high heat until it reaches 350°F on an instant-read thermometer. Carefully add about half the Brussels sprouts (they will bubble and hiss when you add them to the pot) and fry until they float and are nicely golden, about 3 minutes. Use a slotted spoon or frying spider to transfer them to a paper towel–lined plate (some of the leaves may come off the sprouts, which is fine; they're extra delicious and crisp but will probably brown more quickly than the sprouts, so fish them out when they are browned and crisp). Repeat with the remaining Brussels sprouts, sprinkle with the salt and pepper, and serve hot, with the Tahini Sauce on the side for dipping.

MEXICAN AVOCADO

SERVES 4

We always wanted to give people healthy options at Black Tap and now we're learning that the fat in avocado is our friend you don't need an excuse (margarita, anyone?) to eat them. This is like a light, vibrant, chunky guacamole you eat with a fork, no chips needed.

1 TABLESPOON EXTRA-VIRGIN OLIVE OIL

1 TABLESPOON APPLE CIDER VINEGAR

⅛ TEASPOON KOSHER SALT

PINCH OF FRESHLY GROUND BLACK PEPPER

3 AVOCADOS, HALVED, PITTED, PEELED, AND CUT INTO LARGE BITE-SIZE PIECES

¾ CUP PICKLED RED ONIONS (page 72), **COARSELY CHOPPED**

¾ CUP PICO DE GALLO (page 66)

FINELY CHOPPED FRESH CILANTRO, FOR SERVING

1 Whisk together the olive oil, vinegar, salt, and pepper together in a medium bowl. Add the avocado and gently toss to combine.

2 Gently stir in the chopped pickled onions and divide the mixture among four bowls. Top each with some Pico de Gallo and serve sprinkled with cilantro.

FLIP

Honey Maid
HEINZ TOMATO KETCHUP
Jif
Reese's
Nestlé TOLL HOUSE
GOYA
CENTO
SCLAFANI CRUSHED TOMATOES
Jet-Puffed
Kraft
WHIRLY POP
GULDEN'S
Half Sour Pickles
LAMORENA
Wondra
HERSHEY'S

CRAFT BURGERS & CRAZY SHAKES

JOE ISIDORI

CRAFT & CRAZY

PHOTOGRAPHS BY MADONNA+CHILD

BURGERS

FROM

BLACK TAP

SHAKES

PAM KRAUSS BOOKS/AVERY
NEW YORK

CRAZY

SHAKES

Black Tap was always going to have milkshakes, and we've been spinning awesome basic shakes since the day we opened. After all, nothing tastes better with a burger than a milkshake, unless you're having a beer. Black Tap is inspired by nostalgia, and if there is a sweet treat more evocative of being a kid than a milkshake, I don't know what it is.

Just like our burgers, Black Tap shakes were built on the luncheonette classics of my New York childhood; they're easy, drinkable, and topped with lots of whipped cream and a cherry. We start with simple and basic ingredients like a great premium vanilla ice cream and iconic products like Fox's U-bet and Hershey's syrups. They aren't concretes: you don't need a spoon to drink them. We offer nostalgic flavors like chocolate, vanilla, strawberry, coffee, Oreo, peanut butter, cherry, caramel, and Nutella. But I was always messing around in the kitchen, thinking about how to amp them up and make them even more special.

One day my wife, Louise, asked me to make her a "crazy" milkshake. Now, I like to impress my wife, and it's not always easy to do. She's a talented textiles designer, creative, with a sophisticated sensibility. It took me just three months to ask this beautiful, smart, tough woman to marry me. If Louise wanted me to make her a crazy milkshake, I was going to have to get serious. And that's exactly what I did . . . sort of.

What is a crazy shake? It's an extravagant milkshake that's part dessert, part art project. It's stacked with toppings like whole slices of cake or pie or oversized cookies that add height and volume and whose flavors complement and enhance the classic milkshake at its base. It's the candy-covered milkshake of a Willy Wonka fever dream. It's reinventing a childhood basic and making it even better by crafting it well and paying attention to all the sensory details that elevate honest food.

Learning how to construct a crazy shake that stands tall and tastes good was a process of trial and error. It's not easy to cover a milkshake with a bunch of toppings without having it look and taste like a mess. Feel free to conjure up your own images of the delicious fiascos that collapsed and melted on my kitchen counter on the way to these discoveries. Once we learned that commercial cake icing holds embellishments on the rim of the glass better than a lot of other edible "glues," we started adding components to the sides of the shake glasses instead of putting everything on top. We figured out that heavy-bottomed glasses are crucial for balance as the toppings are piled on. Chilling the glasses seemed to cause the icing and whipped cream to seize a bit and made it possible to stud the cream with candies without having them slide away. We experimented with different treats to see what would create the most dramatic effect and also stay put long enough for someone to drink this ephemeral sculpture.

Louise wanted a cotton candy shake because cotton candy is her favorite treat. We started with a strawberry shake for color and flavor. Then we put that shake in a chilled glass rimmed with vanilla icing and coated with metallic, chocolate-covered pearls crowded together so that they looked like they were suspended on air. We piled on the whipped cream and covered it with fluffy tufts of pink and blue cotton candy until it looked like a whimsical cloud, re-creating the big puff you would buy on a stick at a carnival. For sparkle, we put a couple of sticks of rock candy in this concoction. Proudly, I presented it to my wife.

"No," she said as she considered it from all angles, "it's not there yet. It needs something. Maybe you should try sticking a big whirly pop in it?"

Louise is tough, but she's also a genius, with a great eye for color, proportion, and style. (She's a lot like my mother, but that's probably for another book.) One pastel-colored Whirly pop and one photograph later, we posted the cotton candy shake on Instagram, and the rest is history. The Cotton Candy is still our best-selling crazy shake, but it would be my favorite even if it weren't.

At Black Tap, we serve more than one thousand shakes a day, and setting up our stations and glasses in advance is crucial to making sure that every single milkshake looks and tastes great. In between spinning milkshakes, our amazing staff is busy prepping cold glasses, frosting the sides, and studding them with mosaics of M&M's, cookie crumbs, and chocolate pearls so they're ready to go when an order comes in.

The crazy shakes might look baroque, but the elements are pretty basic. If you want to make all your elements from scratch, you can, of course. But you don't have to. Instead, indulge your inner "kid in a candy shop," hit the candy store or the cookie aisle, and stock up on the sweets and treats you love and that make you smile. Go rainbow multihued or stay monochromatic—the choice is yours. Get some heavy glasses and some skewers, if your toppings need them to stay put. Figure out your flavor profile and buy your favorite ice cream, syrup, and some premade cake frosting—Betty Crocker works just fine. Then access your inner artist and go to town.

Making a crazy shake is a fun, creative process. Once you understand the basic method, the shakes are all about combining flavors. You can choose one of my combos, but this

is also your chance to think like a chef. Figure out what you're craving. Let's say you're in the mood to make a peanut butter shake. Think about what goes well with peanut butter: jelly, Fluff, chocolate, and banana are all possibilities. If I decide I want to make a peanut butter and Fluff–inspired treat, maybe I'll try using Fluff as the "glue" on the outside of my milkshake glass. Then I might line up whole mini marshmallows on the side of the glass, or maybe some graham cracker crumbs or banana slices. I'm looking to build layers of flavor. Once I'm happy with the glass and I've actually poured the shake, I can add whipped cream and then look to add texture and flavor with sauces and accessories. In this case, it could be caramel sauce or chocolate syrup, and then maybe salty popcorn or a big Rice Krispies Treat on top. As you go down this path, you'll think of more things that pair well, the taste will evolve, and you will have created your own signature crazy shake.

These shakes have turned out to be a fun way to partner with people and businesses on special projects that highlight their identities, events, products, and ideas. We've designed shakes around the amazing donut from the Brooklyn bakery Dough and my friend Sal's award-winning cupcakes from Little Cupcake Bakeshop in Nolita, and collaborated with our neighbor Otto's Tacos here in SoHo. We made them a horchata milkshake that tasted almost like an icy liquid rice pudding, with cream cheese icing anchoring Cinnamon Toast Crunch cereal crumbs, studded the whipped cream with awesome Mexican-style cookies, and topped the whole thing with a freshly made churro.

If you can't get your hands on freshly fried churros, crazy shakes topped with dramatic slices of cake or pie are easy to plan and execute at home, and I've included recipes to help get you started imagining your own Instagram-worthy creations.

I love running Black Tap, and there are a million moments that make me smile when I'm at work. But my all-time favorite thing is to stand across the bar from a little kid, hand over an amazing-looking foot-tall crazy shake, and watch that kid's face light up like a Christmas tree. That makes my day every time, and I know I'm doing the right thing. I want those kids to remember that magic moment and to bring their own kids to Black Tap to experience it over and over for generations to come. Why not start making some memories of your own.

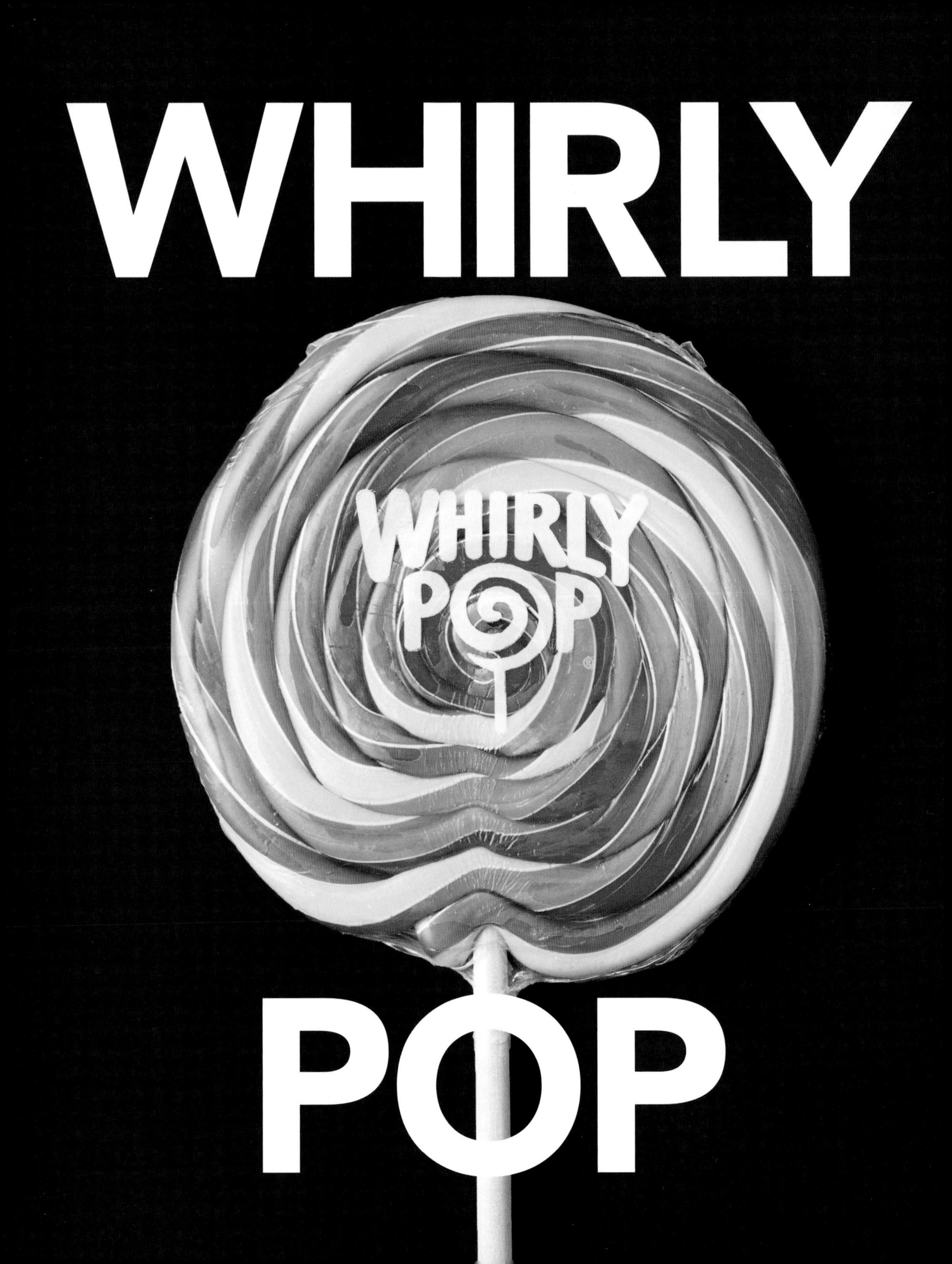
WHIRLY
WHIRLY POP
POP

THE METHOD

Milkshakes are hard to screw up, and even the basic ones will probably make someone very happy. But with a bit of planning and attention to a few small details, you can wow everyone with a crazy shake and enjoy the creative process as much as the final, photo-ready product.

TOOLS

You need tall, heavy-bottomed glasses. We use old-fashioned 16-ounce fountain glasses at Black Tap, but if you have a favorite pint glass, that will usually work well, too. A heavy bottom or some kind of stabilizing foot on the rim is key, because you need it to have enough weight to balance all the crazy toppings you're going to pile on. If you chill the glasses a bit, it will help the toppings adhere and keep the shake cold.

A blender is a necessity for a milkshake, but you don't need anything fancy. We have six milkshake spinners whirring away at Black Tap, but any basic household blender will be just fine. In fact, if you decide to flavor a shake with something chunky, like an actual piece of cake or pie, your blender will probably be more effective and powerful than a professional spinner.

Finally, you'll want a couple of butter knives, long-handled spoons, or skewers to support the larger accessories you plan to use on your crazy shake. The choice will depend on how heavy the big "topper" is, and I specify what I think works best in the recipes that follow.

ICE CREAM

Any premium vanilla ice cream in your supermarket will make a great flavor base and texture for most shakes. Vanilla is all you need for most shakes, because it's easily customizeable and you'll be flavoring it with syrups or other elements. That's right: vanilla ice cream is your blank canvas even if you're making a chocolate or strawberry milkshake, and the flavor will generally be less sweet and overpowering if it comes from chocolate syrup, fresh strawberries, or crumbled-up cookies or another flavor element. Your ice cream should be soft enough to scoop but not melting when you're ready to get to work. Leave it on the counter for 10 minutes or so if it's really hard when you take it out of the freezer.

FROSTING

Black Tap crazy shakes use frosting as the glue that helps the fun stuff adhere to the sides of the glass. Betty Crocker whipped frosting works well, but if there is another brand you especially like, go ahead and try it. Vanilla or chocolate is usually all you need, but I have experimented with lots of other edible "glues," including Nutella, peanut butter, and marshmallow Fluff, and you can, too. The frosting will "hold" better if the glasses are a bit cold when you frost the rims. Absolutely do not use glasses warm from the dishwasher, unless you want a runny mess.

MILK

The purpose of the milk is to loosen up the ice cream and help make it smooth. Some people will tell you that creamier milk makes a creamier shake, but I think the amount of milk in a shake is too small for it to make a big difference. We use whole milk, but you can use whatever kind you have in your fridge.

THE
GLUE

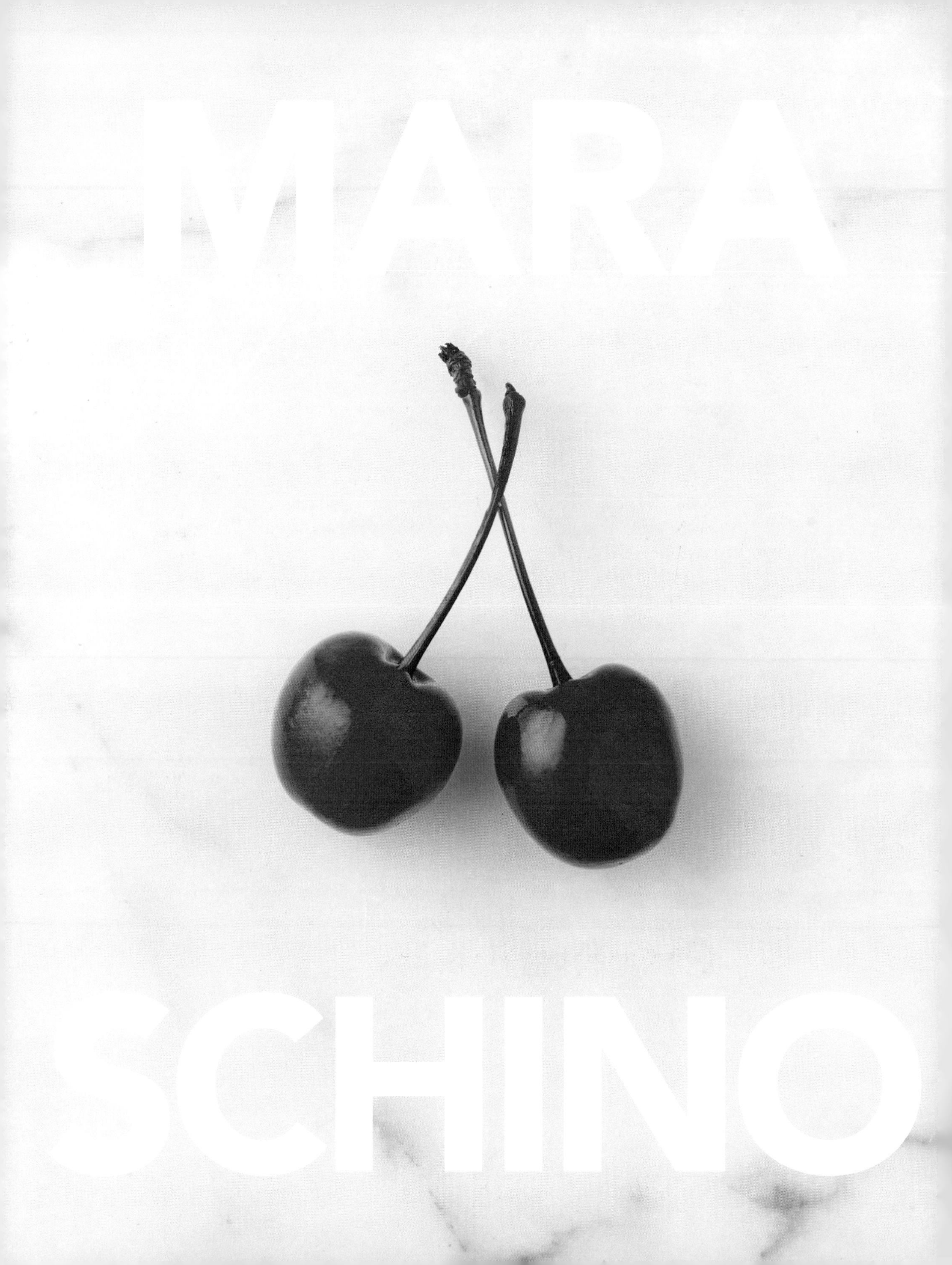
MARA
SCHINO

FLAVORINGS

Most Black Tap shakes are vanilla-based and flavored with some kind of syrup.

We use Hershey's or Fox's chocolate or strawberry syrup, and you can generally find other specialty flavor syrups, like coffee, in large grocery stores or online. You can also flavor with other elements, such as ground espresso, jam, or cake—basically, anything your blender can handle that sounds good to you. We blend Oreo cookies into the Black and White Shake, and flavor the Sweet 'n' Salty with peanut butter. Start small if you decide to flavor this way, because if you blend the shake for too long, it will be too soupy. If you are flavoring with something chunky, like a cookie, crush it before you put it in the blender so that it doesn't prolong the spin.

WHIPPED CREAM

Whipped cream is an important structural element of a crazy shake, because it will support some of your toppings and accessories. We use Reddi-wip, and you should, too. Don't freeze it, but do keep it very cold until you're ready to use it. This will help you get a thick volume on top of your shake. Pile the whipped cream as high as you like.

CHERRIES

Black Tap uses maraschino cherries, just like the luncheonettes whose shakes we grew up on did.

ACCESSORIES

This is the best part! Go to the candy store or the bakery and look for items that are going to complement and enhance the ice cream and flavors you're using. Anything that sounds like a good combination to you is worth trying. I like to have one really dramatic item, like a fat ice cream sandwich, or a giant Pixy Stix, to take things over the top. I usually think about that main accessory first, then choose the trimmings to decorate the side of the glass and the whipped cream afterward. There are no rules here, but I would say four to six elements is a manageable number: one main element, one or two smaller items, like a cookie or Sugar Daddy, then one to three kinds of mini candies to embellish the glass and sprinkle over all.

ROCK
IT

MAKE
IT
RAIN

MAKING THE SHAKE

Our milkshake method is a bit like our burger method: we take a few quality ingredients and handle them as little as possible. The blender creates heat and friction that will make the shake too runny very quickly, so combine your ingredients in the blender jar and spin them for less than a minute. You're looking for a pretty smooth, icy texture that has a little resistance when you pour it or test it with a teaspoon. If it's too thick to pour, add a little more milk and pulse it for just a few seconds. If it's too thin, add a bit more ice cream and, again, give it a brief blend.

PUTTING IT ALL TOGETHER

Serve the shake as soon as possible after you make it, so have a chilled glass that you have already frosted and perhaps studded with candy or cookie crumbs around the rim ready to go before you start to blend. Have the additional decorative elements ready, which means unwrapped, sliced, chopped, crumbled, or sorted by color or size. You don't want your shake to be melting away while you sort M&M's. Then make and pour your shake, take your Reddi-wip out of the fridge, and begin creating. Once you've got the basic technique down, let your imagination roam. You can be inspired by a holiday, an event, a person, or your favorite dessert. We've based milkshakes on caramel apples, black-and-white cookies, candy canes, Hanukkah, the World Series, the Super Bowl, Breast Cancer Awareness, pumpkin pie, and Shark Week—and that's just in the last six months! Get inspired, have fun, express yourself, and make people around you happy.

HERSHEY'S
SYRUP
INDULGENT
CARAMEL FLAVOR
NATURAL AND ARTIFICIAL FLAVOR
FAT FREE
50
CALORIES
PER 1 TBSP
NET WT 22 OZ (1 LB 6 OZ) 623 g
Kraft
Jet-Puffed
MARSHMALLOWS
Have fun with your yum!
10 OCT 2016
22:01
&Creamy
Chocolate
Frosting
NET WT 16 OZ (1 LB) 453g
TOLL HOUSE
SINCE 1939
100% REA
FAT FREE Candy
CHOLESTEROL FREE

SHAKES SHOPPING LIST

- Reddi-wip whipped cream
- Blue Bunny ice cream
- Milk; we use only whole milk at Black Tap but if you prefer you can substitute 2%
- Fox's U-bet chocolate syrup and other flavors as needed
- Hershey's caramel syrup
- Maraschino cherries
- Betty Crocker whipped frostings
- Keebler Soft Batch or Chips Ahoy! chocolate chip cookies
- Sugar Daddies
- Rold Gold pretzel rods
- M&M's, regular and mini sizes
- Reese's Peanut Butter Cups
- Cotton candy
- Rock candy swizzle sticks
- Sixlets candy pearls
- Whirly pops
- Jif peanut butter
- Toll House mini chocolate chips

DRIZZLE

COOKIE SHAKE

MAKES 2 MILKSHAKES

Of all the crazy shakes at Black Tap, this one is the simplest to make. It's also one of the most popular. All milkshakes are a kind of comfort food, but many of the crazy shakes are a little daunting. This vanilla-based shake has a straightforward, almost calming quality, like drinking a giant frozen chocolate chip cookie. Top it with a classic Chipwich to push that illusion even further.

⅓ CUP VANILLA FROSTING

1 CUP PLUS 3 TABLESPOONS FINELY CRUSHED THIN AND CRISPY CHOCOLATE CHIP COOKIES PLUS 2 WHOLE CHOCOLATE CHIP COOKIES

¾ CUP WHOLE MILK

3½ CUPS (20 OUNCES) VANILLA ICE CREAM

CHOCOLATE SYRUP

WHIPPED CREAM

2 CHIPWICH ICE CREAM SANDWICHES

1 Frost the top 1½ inches of two tall 16-ounce glasses with the vanilla frosting. Place 1 cup of the cookie crumbs on a large plate. Use your cupped hand to press the cookie crumbs onto the frosting (or roll the frosted part of the glasses in the crumbs).

2 Combine the milk, ice cream, and remaining 3 tablespoons cookie crumbs in a blender and blend until very smooth, about 1 minute.

3 Squeeze some chocolate syrup along the inside rim of each glass so it drips down the inside of the glass. Divide the shake between the two glasses.

4 Top each shake with whipped cream. Stick a Chipwich on the rim of each glass (you can also insert a long-handled spoon or a butter knife vertically through the center of the ice cream sandwich and then place the end of the spoon or knife in the shake to help the Chipwich stay upright). Stand a chocolate chip cookie upright in the whipped cream. Drizzle more chocolate syrup over the whipped cream, add a straw, and serve immediately.

COTTON CANDY SHAKE

MAKES 2 MILKSHAKES

The original crazy shake looks like what Willy Wonka might make if he came to life in your kitchen. It's an Instagram darling, our best-selling shake, and one of the many reasons I consider my wife a genius. Make it yourself to see what the fuss is all about.

⅓ CUP VANILLA FROSTING

1 CUP SIXLETS CANDY (WE USE A COMBINATION OF WHITE, BLUE, AND PINK)

¾ CUP WHOLE MILK

⅓ CUP STRAWBERRY SYRUP

3½ CUPS (20 OUNCES) VANILLA ICE CREAM

WHIPPED CREAM

COTTON CANDY

2 LARGE LOLLIPOPS

4 ROCK CANDY STICKS

1 Frost the top 1½ inches of two tall 16-ounce glasses with the vanilla frosting. Use your cupped hand to press the Sixlets onto the frosting.

2 Combine the milk, strawberry syrup, and ice cream in a blender and blend until very smooth, about 1 minute. Divide the shake between the two glasses.

3 Top each shake with whipped cream. Pull off puffs of cotton candy and gently place them on the whipped cream. Stick a lollipop and 2 rock candy sticks into each shake, add a straw, and serve immediately.

FLUFFY

COOKIES 'N' CREAM

BLACK AND WHITE SHAKE

MAKES 2 MILKSHAKES

We had this shake, which tastes like a smooth frozen Oreo, on the menu even before we started serving crazy shakes. The flavor reminds me of staying up late as a little kid, waiting for my dad to get home from work. Sharing some Oreos and a glass of milk before bed was our ritual. My mom loves to recall the night she had to call the fire department after I locked her out while she was switching laundry in the basement. They found me, age three, hiding behind the couch with an empty package of Oreos and a big grin. This amped-up version of our Cookies 'n' Cream Shake is garnished with vanilla frosting, Oreo cookie crumbs, and chocolate syrup. Top it with a black-and-white cookie, or use 2 cookies to make an ice cream sandwich topper!

24 OREO COOKIES (12 OUNCES), FINELY CRUSHED OR PULVERIZED IN A FOOD PROCESSOR

⅓ CUP VANILLA FROSTING

¾ CUP WHOLE MILK

3½ CUPS (20 OUNCES) VANILLA ICE CREAM

CHOCOLATE SYRUP

WHIPPED CREAM

1 CUP MINI MARSHMALLOWS

2 BLACK-AND-WHITE COOKIES

1 Place ½ cup of the crushed Oreos in a blender and spread the rest out in an even layer on a large plate.

2 Frost the top 1½ inches of two 16-ounce glasses with the frosting. Press some of the crushed Oreos into the frosting on each glass (you should have some leftover for decorating; if not, crush up a couple more cookies).

3 Add the milk and ice cream to the Oreos in the blender and blend until smooth, about 1 minute.

4 Squeeze some chocolate syrup along the inside rim of each glass so it drips down the inside of the glass. Divide the shake between the two glasses.

5 Top each shake with whipped cream, the mini marshmallows, and the leftover crushed Oreos. Stick a black-and-white cookie on the rim of each glass. Serve immediately.

SWEET 'N' SALTY SHAKE

MAKES 2 MILKSHAKES

When I was a kid, my aunt Theresa used to take me and my cousins to the movies and let us get Whoppers, Jujubes, and popcorn. She's the best. We would dump the candy right into the popcorn buckets and go to town. That combination of sweet and salty is a great flavor profile. The salty/sweet here comes from peanut butter and pretzels studded with a riot of all your favorite stuff: M&M's, Reese's cups, and Sugar Daddies.

⅓ CUP CHOCOLATE FROSTING

½ CUP REGULAR-SIZE M&M'S

6 MINI PEANUT BUTTER CUPS

¾ CUP WHOLE MILK

6 TABLESPOONS SMOOTH PEANUT BUTTER

3½ CUPS (20 OUNCES) VANILLA ICE CREAM

CHOCOLATE SYRUP

WHIPPED CREAM

MINI M&M'S

4 PRETZEL RODS

2 SUGAR DADDY CANDIES, UNWRAPPED

2 CHOCOLATE-COVERED PRETZELS

1 Frost the top 1½ inches of two tall 16-ounce glasses with the chocolate frosting. Stick the regular-size M&M's onto the icing and press 3 peanut butter cups onto the rim of each glass.

2 Combine the milk, peanut butter, and ice cream in a blender and blend until very smooth, about 2 minutes. Squeeze some chocolate syrup onto the inside rim of each glass, letting the syrup drip down the inside of the glass. Divide the shake between the two glasses.

3 Top each shake with whipped cream, drizzle with chocolate syrup, and sprinkle with mini M&M's. Stick two pretzel rods and a Sugar Daddy into each glass. Place a chocolate-covered pretzel on each and serve immediately.

NUTTY

BKLYN

BROOKLYN BLACKOUT SHAKE

MAKES 2 MILKSHAKES

Sal, the owner of Little Cupcake Bakeshop, where I get coffee every day, is from Brooklyn. I'm from the Bronx. Most mornings you can find us at a table with our heads together in the great tradition of two Italian-Americans having a sit-down on the margins of old Little Italy, but the only deals we ever make involve desserts. Sal's award-winning blackout cake was the perfect New York inspiration for this chocolate shake, developed to commemorate the opening of Black Tap Down, the basement dining room we built out underneath our original SoHo bar.

6 TABLESPOONS CHOCOLATE FROSTING

1 CUP MINI CHOCOLATE CHIPS, PLUS MORE FOR DECORATING

¾ CUP PLUS 2 TABLESPOONS WHOLE MILK

3½ CUPS (20 OUNCES) VANILLA ICE CREAM

⅓ CUP CHOCOLATE SYRUP, PLUS EXTRA FOR DECORATING

WHIPPED CREAM

2 BROOKLYN BLACKOUT CUPCAKES OR CHOCOLATE-FROSTED CHOCOLATE CUPCAKES

1 Frost the top 1½ inches of two tall 16-ounce glasses with the chocolate frosting. Press the chocolate chips into the frosting all around the glasses.

2 Combine the milk, ice cream, and chocolate syrup in a blender and blend until creamy, about 1 minute.

3 Squeeze some chocolate syrup along the inside rim of each glass so it drips down the inside of the glass. Divide the shake between the two glasses.

4 Top each shake with whipped cream and more chocolate chips, and drizzle with chocolate syrup. Peel off the cupcake paper and press the cupcake onto the rim of each glass (you can also insert a long-handled spoon or butter knife vertically through the center of the cupcake and then place the end of the spoon or knife in the shake to help the cupcake stay upright). Add a straw and serve immediately.

RED VELVET SHAKE

MAKES 2 MILKSHAKES

This is a Valentine's Day special. People wait on a winter line for hours with their partner to take a picture of themselves sharing this dramatic shake. It's a chocolate-and-Oreo-based shake, adorned with Hershey's Kisses and red M&M's, and topped with a fat slice of red velvet cake. Serve it with two straws, obviously.

⅓ CUP CHOCOLATE FROSTING
20 HERSHEY'S KISSES, UNWRAPPED
30 RED M&M'S
¾ CUP WHOLE MILK
3½ CUPS (20 OUNCES) VANILLA ICE CREAM
3 TABLESPOONS CHOCOLATE SYRUP, PLUS EXTRA FOR DECORATING
4 OREO COOKIES, CRUSHED INTO SMALL PIECES
WHIPPED CREAM
2 SLICES RED VELVET CAKE

1 Frost the top 1½ inches of two tall 16-ounce glasses with the chocolate frosting. Press the Kisses into the frosting on each glass, then fill in the spaces between them with the M&M's.

2 Combine the milk, ice cream, chocolate syrup, and crushed Oreos in a blender and blend until very smooth, about 1 minute.

3 Squeeze some chocolate syrup along the inside rim of each glass so it drips down the inside of the glass. Divide the shake between the two glasses.

4 Top each shake with whipped cream. Drizzle with chocolate syrup. Top with a slice of cake and drizzle with more chocolate sauce.

LOVE

BOOM
FOX'S
u-bet
ORIGINAL
KD
CHOCOLATE
FLAVOR SYRUP
NET WT 22 OZ (1 LB 6 OZ) 624 g
FAT FREE

DONUT SHAKE

MAKES 2 MILKSHAKES

Coffee and donuts is a timeless flavor pairing that we've done one better in this shake. We stud the chocolate frosting with Whoppers to add a crisp, airy, wafer texture, and top it with a donut. We use a Café au Lait donut from Dough, a great bakery in BedStuy, Brooklyn, but a classic glazed or vanilla-frosted donut would work just as nicely. You could also use Nutella for the glue here; it's not as sticky as regular frosting, but it tastes great if you don't mind a bit of a mess.

⅓ CUP CHOCOLATE FROSTING
60 WHOPPERS
¾ CUP WHOLE MILK
3½ CUPS (20 OUNCES) VANILLA ICE CREAM
3 TABLESPOONS COFFEE SYRUP, SUCH AS FOX'S U-BET
WHIPPED CREAM
CHOCOLATE SPRINKLES
CHOCOLATE SYRUP
2 DONUTS OF YOUR CHOICE

1 Frost the upper 1½ inches of two tall 16-ounce glasses. Press the Whoppers into the frosting.

2 Combine the milk, ice cream, and coffee syrup in a blender and blend until very smooth, about 1 minute.

3 Squeeze some coffee syrup along the inside rim of each glass so it drips down the inside of the glass. Divide the shake between the two glasses.

4 Top each shake with whipped cream and the sprinkles. Drizzle with chocolate syrup. Insert a long-handled spoon or a butter knife through the center of the donut and then place the end of the spoon or knife in the shake so the donut rests upright in the whipped cream. Drizzle with more chocolate syrup, add a straw, and serve immediately.

BLUEBERRY PIE SHAKE

MAKES 2 MILKSHAKES

When Chase Bank asked us to develop a shake for Pi Day, we experimented with a lot of different flavors and ways to highlight pie in a milkshake. As with so many things, simple turned out to be best. We flavored a vanilla shake with a homemade blueberry coulis (at home you can drain the liquid from a can of syrup-packed blueberries) and adorned it with pie crust crumbs. A big piece of blueberry pie made even more dramatic by an à la mode garnish was the perfect finishing touch. We sliced the pie in two and stacked the pieces for maximum height and effect.

⅓ CUP VANILLA FROSTING

½ CUP CRUSHED GRAHAM CRACKERS (ABOUT 8 GRAHAM CRACKER SQUARES)

¾ CUP WHOLE MILK

3½ CUPS (20 OUNCES) VANILLA ICE CREAM, PLUS 2 SCOOPS FOR SERVING

¼ CUP LIQUID FROM CANNED BLUEBERRIES PACKED IN SYRUP, PLUS EXTRA SYRUP FOR DECORATING

WHIPPED CREAM

2 SLICES OF BLUEBERRY PIE

FRESH BLUEBERRIES FOR GARNISH

1 Frost the top 1½ inches of two tall 16-ounce glasses with the frosting. Press the graham cracker crumbs into the frosting.

2 Combine the milk, ice cream, and ¼ cup blueberry syrup in a blender and blend until very smooth, about 1 minute. Divide the shake between the two glasses.

3 Top each shake with whipped cream. Drizzle with more blueberry syrup. Insert a long-handled spoon or a butter knife vertically through the pie and then place the end of the spoon or knife in the shake so the pie rests in the whipped cream. Place a scoop of ice cream on each. Sprinkle with fresh blueberries. Add a straw and serve immediately.

A LA
MODE

TOASTED

S'MORES SHAKE

MAKES 2 MILKSHAKES

This one is nostalgic and comforting. It's a chocolate shake garnished with marshmallow Fluff and studded with graham cracker crumbs and tiny marshmallows, so you're getting the s'mores flavor combination from several directions. Oversized homemade s'mores are the natural—and eye-catching—topper. This is a good one to serve in mini portions, too; divide one shake among three 8-ounce mason jars and garnish away!

⅓ CUP VANILLA FROSTING
1 CUP MINI MARSHMALLOWS
3 TABLESPOONS FINE GRAHAM CRACKER CRUMBS
¾ CUP PLUS 2 TABLESPOONS WHOLE MILK
3½ CUPS (20 OUNCES) VANILLA ICE CREAM
8 GRAHAM CRACKER SQUARES
8 LARGE MARSHMALLOWS
4 SQUARES OF A HERSHEY'S CHOCOLATE BAR
3 TABLESPOONS CHOCOLATE SYRUP, PLUS EXTRA FOR DECORATING
WHIPPED CREAM

1 Frost the top 1½ inches of two tall 16-ounce glasses. Press the mini marshmallows into the frosting all the way around the glass, then sprinkle with about half the graham crumbs.

2 Combine the milk, ice cream, and 3 tablespoons of the graham cracker crumbs in a blender and blend until very smooth, about 1 minute.

3 While the shake blends, make the s'mores: Heat the broiler to high and adjust an oven rack to the upper-middle position. Place 4 graham cracker squares on a sheet of aluminum foil, then place a large marshmallow on top of each cracker. Place the baking sheet in the oven and broil until the marshmallow is golden brown, 30 to 45 seconds (broiler intensities vary, so watch the marshmallows closely). Remove the baking sheet from the oven and press a square of chocolate directly onto the marshmallow. Set a second graham cracker square on top of each.

4 Squeeze some chocolate syrup along the inside rim of each glass so it drips down the inside of the glass. Divide the shake between the two glasses.

5 Top each shake with whipped cream and drizzle with chocolate syrup. Set two s'mores on top of each shake, add a straw, and serve immediately.

SOUR POWER MILKSHAKE

MAKES 2 MILKSHAKES

I am a Sour Patch fanatic. When Disney Channel star Zendaya asked Black Tap to host her album release party and create a crazy shake for the occasion, it was an opportunity for me to experiment with my favorite candy. This black cherry–based shake decorated like a rainbow was an instant hit. We use special sour gummy poppers to adorn the glasses, but you can use regular Sour Patch Kids, too. This has an especially dramatic presentation with a skewered rainbow-striped sour belt and a giant Pixy Stix. I love it when kids order the "Sour POWER!" with a shout and a fist pump.

2 SOUR BELTS, DIVIDED INTO THIRDS CROSSWISE

⅓ CUP VANILLA FROSTING

½ POUND SOUR GUMMY POPPERS

¾ CUP WHOLE MILK

⅓ CUP CHERRY ICE CREAM TOPPING (YOU CAN ALSO USE THE LIQUID FROM CHERRIES CANNED IN SYRUP)

3½ CUPS (20 OUNCES) VANILLA ICE CREAM

WHIPPED CREAM

NERDS, FOR SPRINKLING

2 RAINBOW TWIST LOLLIPOPS

2 LARGE PIXY STIX

1 Trim two long wooden skewers so they are no more than 3 inches taller than your glasses. Shape each sour belt segment into a circle and slide 3 onto each skewer.

2 Frost the top 1½ inches of each glass with the vanilla frosting. Stick the sour gummy poppers onto the glass.

3 Combine the milk, cherry topping, and ice cream in a blender and blend until very smooth, about 1 minute.

4 Divide the shake between the two glasses. Top each with whipped cream and sprinkle with Nerds. Stick the sour belt skewer into the glass along with the lollipops and Pixy Stix, add a straw, and serve immediately.

SOUR POWER

XOXO

BIRTHDAY CAKE SHAKE

MAKES 2 MILKSHAKES

You may have served ice cream on your cake, but this shake stands that formula on its head! The bigger, the better in this case, because we've found that larger cake slices balance nicely on the rim of the glass and make a dramatic presentation, especially showered with sprinkles and/or topped with a sparkler. We generally make this with a vanilla-based milkshake and classic white or yellow cake with vanilla frosting, but this is a perfect over-the-top celebration shake to customize for your guest of honor with his or her favorite birthday cake.

⅓ CUP VANILLA FROSTING
36 LARGE WHITE NONPAREIL WAFERS
¾ CUP PLUS 2 TABLESPOONS WHOLE MILK
3½ CUPS (20 OUNCES) VANILLA ICE CREAM
¼ CUP MARSHMALLOW FLUFF
2½ SLICES BIRTHDAY CAKE
WHIPPED CREAM
RAINBOW SPRINKLES
MARASCHINO CHERRIES

1 Frost the top 1½ inches of two tall 16-ounce glasses. Press the nonpareil wafers into the frosting on each glass.

2 Combine the milk, ice cream, Fluff, and the half slice of birthday cake (a little less than ½ cup of cake) in a blender and blend until very smooth, about 1 minute.

3 Divide the shake between the two glasses.

4 Top each shake with whipped cream and sprinkles. Insert a long-handled spoon or a butter knife vertically through the center of each piece of cake and then place the end of the spoon or knife in the shake so the cake rests in the whipped cream. Top with more whipped cream and a cherry. Add a straw and serve immediately (candles optional!).

IT

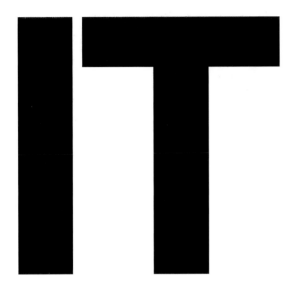

FLIP